Classic Movie
COMEDIANS

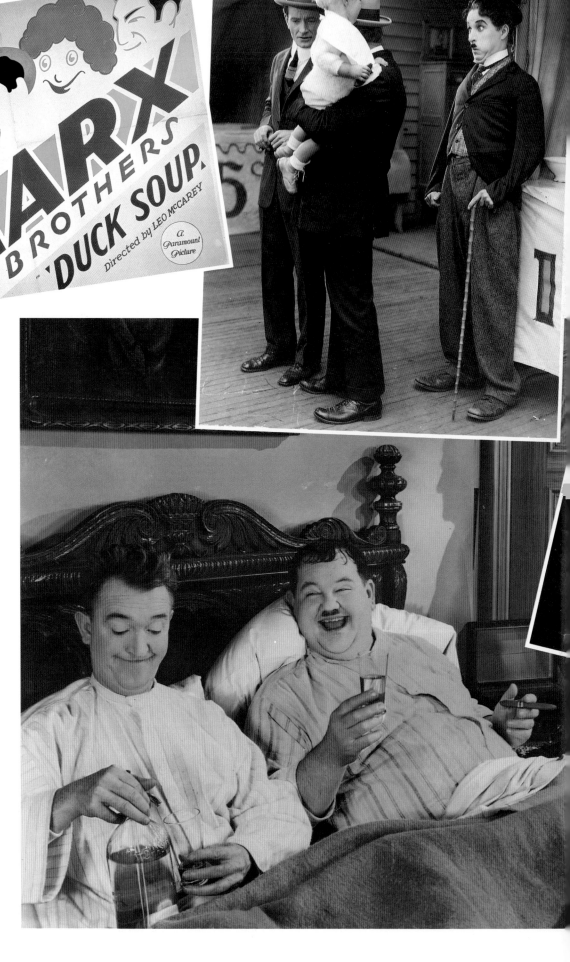

PREVIOUS PAGE,
CLOCKWISE FROM TOP: Laurel and Hardy in *Men o' War*; Charlie Chaplin in *Easy Street*; The Marx Brothers; Buster Keaton in *Frozen North*; Harold Lloyd in *Movie Crazy*; W C Fields in *You Can't Cheat an Honest Man*.

THESE PAGES,
CLOCKWISE FROM ABOVE: A poster for the Marx Brothers in *Duck Soup*; Charlie Chaplin in *The Circus*; Harold Lloyd in *Safety Last*; a poster for Buster Keaton in *The General*; W C Fields in *My Little Chickadee*; Laurel and Hardy in *A Chump at Oxford*.

Classic Movie COMEDIANS

NEIL SINYARD

BISON GROUP

CONTENTS

First published in 1992 by
Bison Books Ltd
Kimbolton House
117A Fulham Road
London SW3 6RL

ISBN 0 86124 878 3

Printed in Hong Kong

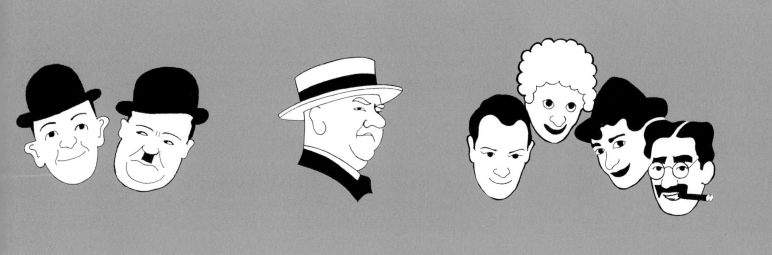

INTRODUCTION

There is a verse that runs roughly as follows:

> They told him it could not be done;
> That if he tried, he'd rue it.
> But he tried that thing that could not be done –
> And he couldn't do it.

The British actor Richard Briers has said that, for him, those lines contain the essence of comedy. They are about the gap between aspiration and attainment, the will and the deed. Comedy explores the contradiction between what people want and what they do. It is about people who, against all advice and all odds, set out to do something – and don't do it. One can almost see Laurel and Hardy trying absurdly and in vain to get that piano up a vast flight of steps in *The Music Box*.

Like Mia Farrow in Woody Allen's *The Purple Rose of Cairo*, all of us have to come to terms with the fact that the champagne we expected from our lives might taste no better than ginger ale. If we love the comedians, the reason is that they put life's inevitable disappointments into some sort of proportion. They take on our inadequacies and, by extending and exaggerating them, they relieve us of their burden by making us feel momentarily superior. Nobody could be quite as incompetent as Laurel and Hardy, we sigh with relief and gratitude, nor quite as gullible as Tony Hancock, say. Comedians are the bravest of performers because they invite our laughter and are not afraid to look foolish. They accommodate, for our benefit, the infinite registers of failure: the inevitability of failure (Laurel and Hardy); the resilience of failure (Chaplin); the stoical dignity of failure (Buster Keaton); and even (in a waspish self-portrait like Woody Allen's *Stardust Memories*) the failure of success.

What is interesting here is the closeness of comedy to despair, which is the reason that so many great comedians (Chaplin, Keaton, W C Fields) have been either serious, self-destructive, or misanthropic personalities for whom comedy has been a safety-valve of sanity. After all, a laugh is only a gasp in reverse. Chaplin's basic rule for screen direction was 'long shot for comedy, close-up for tragedy,' as if the only real difference between them was distance and point of view. Small wonder that

ABOVE RIGHT: The poster for Chaplin's *The Circus*.

BELOW RIGHT: W C Fields with Gracie Allen (right) in *International House* (1932).

LEFT: Stan Laurel (above) and Oliver Hardy (below) in their Oscar-winning short, *The Music Box*.

6

"On your way out pick up a stepladder"

a common image for so many of the great comedians – Chaplin, Keaton, Laurel and Hardy – is the walk across the tightrope: it requires perfect balance and one false step can send you toppling into the abyss. Maybe one difference between a classic comedian and a merely competent one is that whereas comedy for the latter is a luxury, comedy for the former is a life-line.

'What a sad business being funny,' says the ballerina to Chaplin's clown in *Limelight*, to which he replies: 'Very sad, if they don't laugh.' The absence of laughter is a kind of death, and when a comic fails, his act is significantly said to have 'died.' At the end of his life the old actor Edmund Gwenn told a friend that he thought even dying was less hard than playing comedy. There was something about the perverse psychology of comedy that always terrified Harry Langdon. Why was it that people loved to laugh yet it was the hardest thing to make them do, whereas they hated to cry yet could do so seemingly at the drop of

a hat? Why is comedy so often under-valued compared with drama or tragedy? Sadly reflecting on the way Laurel and Hardy comedies had so often been trashed by the critics, Jerry Lewis thought the reason was that 'people fear comedy. Because the truth of it is like a bone coming through the skin.'

Lewis's comment might seem melodra-matic, but there is a sense in which, when watching the dazzling desperation of a Chaplin, the guttural grumbles of a Fields, the astringent anarchy of the Marx Brothers, one can feel its validity. All of them are making a comment, frequently unflattering, on the state of things, so-called normal society, what is laughingly called the human condition. The comic is often the enemy of the values by which most people are compelled to live their lives, which means that, at their greatest, their insights course through an audience like a tonic serum. George Orwell once observed that 'whatever is funny is sub-versive,' because a joke is 'a sort of mental rebellion, a momentary wish that things were otherwise.' The comic embodies pre-cisely those things that society spends most of its time discouraging: the shabby, the lazy, the cowardly, and the dishonest. We respond to this because we recognize it as a side to ourselves which, however hard we suppress it, is always there, and there-fore we enjoy our rebellion against virtue; as Orwell says, 'human beings want to be good, but not too good, and not quite all the time.'

Who, for example, has not been tempted to disturb an elaborate display in a super-market, a row of cans meticulously piled one on top of the other? Jerry Lewis does it in *The Disorderly Orderly*, and in a way takes us right back to the manic antics of the Key-stone Kops that practically originated screen comedy for most film audiences. Comedy can give us the vicarious thrill of destruction and chaos, as the custard-pie has demonstrated down the decades. But it can go further, becoming a means of striking back at all the enemies of progress, individual or social. These can be identified in entirely different ways: for Chaplin they are the police, the pompous, the bureaucrat, the authoritarian; for Fields, the enemies are sentiment, children, womanhood, family life, bourgeois respectability. But it is significant that Eastern European film-makers recognized that the best weapon against totalitarianism was comedy. Laughter not only disarms but is an explosion of recognition that makes it impossible to deny a work's essential truth. Laughter knocks the scissors out of a censor's hands. Milos Forman, who made that great black comedy *The Fireman's Ball* in Czechoslovakia in 1967, said: 'sometimes truth is not enough: it must be a truth that *surprises*.'

Comedy is a surprise. The seventeenth-century philosopher Thomas Hobbes defined laughter as 'the expression of a sudden glory.' He felt that it came for an audience either through 'some sudden act that pleaseth them' (that is, they identified or sympathized with this act) or through the 'apprehension of some deformed thing in another, by comparison whereof they suddenly applaud themselves' (that is, they felt superior). The critic V F Perkins

LEFT: 'Is this a game of chance?' 'Not the way I play it.' W C Fields deals a shady hand in *My Little Chickadee*.

ABOVE: Peter Sellers (left), in his first portrayal of Inspector Clouseau, and David Niven (right) in *The Pink Panther*.

LEFT: Give a dog a bone: Chaplin in *The Gold Rush*.

has used this as a basis for usefully distinguishing between two types of film clown: those whose triumphs we share (the mouse Jerry, Chaplin, Keaton, The Marx Brothers, Harold Lloyd) and those whose humiliations we enjoy (Tom the cat, Laurel and Hardy, Jerry Lewis, Peter Sellers as Inspector Clouseau). While acknowledging that these are not absolute distinctions – Chaplin and Keaton do not always triumph, Laurel and Lewis do not always fail – Perkins argues that, on one level, it is a distinction between those comedians whom we laugh *with* and those whom we laugh *at*. It is only one of many distinctions that could be made. There is also the distinction between the introvert comedian (eg Woody Allen) and the extrovert comedian (eg Mel Brooks), which translates into different subjects for comedy, the former concerned with individual inadequacies and disappointment, the latter with basic human concerns and needs, like hunger, greed, and love. One might even see it in different terms, suggesting that whereas the humor of introvert comedy comes from an inability to relate to the world around you, the humor of extrovert comedy comes more from an

attack launched on that world. Laurel and Hardy are doves, mainly being put upon; the Marx Brothers are hawks, carrying the fight to the enemy, warriors of wit.

This survey of classic movie comedians is obviously partial and selective, in its emphasis on performers more than on directors or writers, say, and its emphasis on the period between 1920 and 1950 when the cinema was the most popular form of mass entertainment and where people

used to go to forget their troubles. During the silent era, comedy was king, and the techniques of pantomime and slapstick were brought to a new pitch of inventiveness by a uniquely gifted clutch of clowns eager to master this fascinating new medium. When sound came, a new breed of comic anarchist emerged, mocking society's sacred cows with an often brilliant barrage of audacious verbal wit.

But of what did their greatness consist? What is it that makes a movie comedian a 'classic,' whose work survives long after his death? A recent television bio-pic of Tony Hancock, called *Hancock* (1991), more or less implied that Hancock's attempt to find the answer to that question by reading weighty theoretical tomes on the topic by Freud, Bergson, and others, was one of the things that caused his decline and hastened his suicide. From experience, brilliant comedy technicians like Stan Laurel

ABOVE: Poster for W C Fields in the 1936 film *Poppy*.

and Groucho Marx knew what worked with audiences, but they always drew back from theorizing about why audiences found certain things funny.

Thinking about the classic comedians in this volume, one can only say that occasionally one has been struck by a certain resemblance of background. They all came up the hard way, either in retreat from a harsh childhood (Chaplin, Keaton, Fields) or through a delayed recognition of their quality (Lloyd, Langdon, Laurel and Hardy, the Marx Brothers). In most cases it made them tough enough to survive, but it also meant they acquired the grit, the technique, and an essential knowledge of their craft and of themselves. Nearly all of them accumulated experience in vaudeville or music hall before working in films, which gave them a ready repertoire on which to draw for the movies, and honed their technique. They were all perfectionists, working tirelessly to make the virtually impossible seem inevitable and natural. Finally, and perhaps most importantly, they were all completely individualistic, discovering a 'form' and a 'character' that belonged to them and to nobody else. In turn this 'character' seemed to reflect some basic

truth about human nature and so struck a responsive and lasting chord with audiences. Comedy, after all, is an exposure of what it is to be human. These comedians became and remain classics because they found an exquisite balance between foolishness and humanity. They make us laugh at life, without depriving it of its dignity and its value. They reconcile us to its (and our) follies and foibles. They help us recognize who we are.

CHAPTER ONE

Charlie Chaplin

CHARLIE CHAPLIN

To some, he was Charlie, to others Charlot, or Carlino, or Carlos, or Carlitos. Because of the new invention of movies he became more famous more quickly than any other comedian – indeed any other personality – in the history of the world. It happened through his creation of a character dressed in rags but forever dreaming of being a gentleman, a poet, a prince. Charlie Chaplin's Tramp remains to this day the most instantly identifiable film character ever created.

No more extraordinary talent than Chaplin's has ever graced the cinema. 'He is the Adam from whom we are all descended,' said the great Italian director, Federico Fellini. 'He is beyond praise because he is the greatest of them all,' commented the darling of the *nouvelle vague*, Jean-Luc Godard. 'The master of masters, the film-maker of film-makers,' was the opinion of the French film director, Jean Renoir. Note that these disciples of Chaplin are regarded as high-brow, avant-garde, intellectual directors. One of Chaplin's most extraordinary feats was the breadth of his appeal. There was no more cynical and iconoclastic commentator and wit than Alexander Woolcott, but even he said of Chaplin that he would be prepared to

defend the proposition that this 'darling of the mob,' as he put it, was also the 'foremost living artist.'

Yet amid all this it still seems possible to underestimate the immensity of his achievement, and momentarily to take him for granted. It should never be forgotten that his life was the most extraordinary rags-to-riches story of the twentieth century, and that Chaplin's universal success came out of a childhood that bore a strong resemblance to a Victorian horror story. Most people, and most comics, would have been glad enough to survive that and would have drawn a discreet veil over it as success came. But Chaplin did not just refuse to disown this background: in his work he returned to it again and again, insistently reminding society of the poor and the dispossessed and also, in the Tramp's defiance of society, showing their resilience and courage.

LEFT: Charlie Chaplin crosses the Atlantic to make his name in France, where they called him Charlot.

LEFT BELOW: The Tramp tries to sneak an abandoned baby into a nearby pram in *The Kid*.

RIGHT: A vivid poster advertising Chaplin's *The Adventurer* in 1917.

But he went even further than that. There was a strong relation between comedy and autobiography in Chaplin's work, not only in the way his life inspired his comedy, but also in the way his comedy was a means of coming to terms with aspects of both his early and later life (the poverty of his early years, the political persecution of his maturity) which otherwise could have embittered him or driven him mad. There was also always a strong relation between comedy and pathos in Chaplin. His great comic creation, the Tramp, was almost a tragic hero – a decent man at the mercy of destiny and a cruel and corrupt society, but who keeps bobbing up like a cork on a tide, too quick-witted for the bullies and the bureaucrats, refusing to submit to his persecutors. Of all the great comedians, Chaplin is the one who most clearly makes us consider the proximity of comedy to tragedy.

Chaplin dared. He was the most versatile of physical comedians and an honestly envious W C Fields had to concede that 'he's the best ballet dancer that ever lived, and if I get a good chance, I'll kill him with my bare hands.' But straight comedy was not enough. He wanted people to laugh but he also wanted them to cry, to feel, to think – above all, to change. Chaplin spoke out against social injustice. In *The Great Dictator* (1940) he satirized and ridiculed

ABOVE RIGHT: Charlie Chaplin and the blind flower-girl (Virginia Cherrill) in *City Lights*.

RIGHT: Chaplin discovered with 'Scraps' in *A Dog's Life* (1918).

Nazism at a time when America was pursuing a policy of cautious isolationism and, in the anti-Communist hysteria of the postwar period, Chaplin's radical political views, not to mention lurid stories of his romantic entanglements, got him into deep trouble. Once the best-loved man in America, he became the most hated. Chaplin was not a Communist, but a 'peacemonger' as he put it – 'the god of non-violence' was Renoir's phrase for him – yet, under intense pressure he nevertheless refused to tailor his opinions to the climate of the time. 'He lived totally without fear,' said the actress Louise Brooks. When, in *The King of New York* (1957), he became the first film-maker to speak out explicitly against the McCarthy era in America, Roberto Rossellini, the father of Italian neo-realism, expressed the heartfelt sentiments of many when he praised the film as 'the work of a truly free man.'

Reginald Gardner (left), Charlie Chaplin (center) and Henry Daniell (right) exude absurd authority in *The Great Dictator*.

Throughout his career Chaplin was plagued by people determined to denigrate his character and undermine his achievement. Who now cares whether Chaplin originated the idea of the Tramp, when he is undoubtedly the actor who immortalized it? When Buster Keaton was invited to complain about his treatment on Chaplin's *Limelight* (1952) and to argue that he was underpaid, Buster growled: 'Underpaid? I would have worked with Chaplin for nothing.' Over the last 20 years or so, Chaplin's reputation has taken a hammering from a number of critics but, to those who have suggested that Chaplin was 'overrated,' the writer Sean French has a wonderfully contemptuous riposte: 'When I hear a critic say that, I feel as if a molehill has said that Mount Everest's reputation for height was undeserved.' Chaplin is to the cinema quite simply what Dickens is to the novel, and to popular imagination: the

17

most universal, inventive, and many-sided of creative artists, who could simultaneously soar to the highest reaches of his art while also giving the public what they wanted. To understand Chaplin and his comedy fully it is necessary to know something of his 'Dickensian' childhood. Born in 1889, Chaplin was brought up in Victorian London by parents who were minor music-hall performers. His father was an alcoholic who separated from the family when Chaplin was a boy and died soon afterwards. His mother suffered a mental breakdown which led to her being confined for long periods in a workhouse asylum. With his elder half-brother, Sydney, Chaplin spent much of his early life in the poor-house. Like Dickens (whose own father was imprisoned for debt), Chaplin was haunted by what he saw as family disgrace and, to survive, was thrown onto his own resources. Also like Dickens he compensated for his lonely childhood by acting out imaginary personages, as well as characters from books.

Small wonder then that Chaplin's favorite novel to the end of his life was Dickens's *Oliver Twist*, whose workhouse scenes must have been so evocative of his own childhood. Small wonder also that Chaplin should fix on the figure of the Tramp as his comic persona or *alter ego*, for he knew well that destitute life and had seen such figures from personal experience. Neither is it surprising that, even at the height of his fame, he felt insecurity, recalling humiliation and poverty, and feeling, he said, 'no different at heart from the unhappy and defeated men, the failures.' To the end of his life, justifiably or not, he had the reputation of being mean with money, but if so it would be understandable and another example of how deeply his childhood had scarred him. Poverty and hunger are the guiding themes of most of his films. In one of Chaplin's greatest successes, *The Kid* (1921), the Tramp's cramped living quarters were consciously modeled after the attic where Charlie lived as a child and where, on waking up in the morning, he could remember always bumping his head on the ceiling.

His performing gifts became apparent

RIGHT: Chaplin in a scene from his bucolic comedy *Sunnyside* (1919).

ABOVE: The promised land: Chaplin, Edna Purviance (center) and Kitty Bradbury (right) arrive in America in *The Immigrant*.

when he was discovered doing impersonations of Dickens's characters. They were actually impersonations of actors whom he had seen doing Dickensian impersonations, for at that time Chaplin could barely read. Once again like Dickens, Chaplin had a life-long regret and inferiority complex about his lack of formal education and was to compensate with an extraordinary self-education program, in which he read everything he could lay his hands on, from literature to philosophy, from languages to politics. 'He became a self-made aristocrat,' Louise Brooks said of him.

He joined Fred Karno's famous pantomime and music-hall troupe and rapidly became their star performer, touring America with them in 1910. When America came into view, Stan Laurel remembered Chaplin rushing to the railings of the cattle boat on which they were traveling and shouting: 'America, I am coming to con-

quer you! Every man, woman and child shall have my name on their lips – Charles Spencer Chaplin!' It is fascinating to speculate on the significance of this. America must have seemed a land of opportunity after his traumatic upbringing in London. Chaplin was to say that he felt immediately at home in the States, 'a foreigner among foreigners,' as he put it. Yet he never became an American citizen, a fact that was to become a bone of contention when he was being hounded for his political views in the late 1940s and early 1950s. 'I am a citizen of the world,' he would always say. And yet if there is a single image in a Chaplin movie more memorable than any other, it is probably that extraordinary moment in *The Immigrant* (1917), when the immigrants crowd on the deck for their first view of the Statue of Liberty but are suddenly roped off together like cattle by insensitive customs officials. A land of opportunity, indeed,

but not without its ominous side and not without exacting its own price.

Spotted by Mack Sennett, Chaplin was invited to join Sennett's Keystone unit. He did so somewhat reluctantly, tempted by the money. But at that time he still preferred live theater, aspired to be a serious actor, and felt, moreover, that he did not fit into Sennett's madcap style, where frenzy was the order of the day and the chase took precedence over character. According to Chaplin it was one afternoon, when he was searching for an alternative character, to distinguish him from other Sennett performers, that the Tramp came into being. In the costume department he discovered a pair of outsize trousers, a derby, a tight coat, a cane, a pair of floppy shoes and a little brush-like moustache. All he needed to add was a funny shuffling walk that he remembered from an old peddler he had seen in his youth on the London streets who walked that way because his shoes were too small. Essentially, on that one afternoon, the best-known character in film history was born.

But, of course, it was what Chaplin was to make of the character that was import-

ABOVE: Ready to give chase: the Keystone Kops. While with Mack Sennett, Chaplin was to react against the frenzy of the Keystone style.

LEFT: Chaplin in *The Circus*.

ant. For Chaplin the character was 'many-sided – a tramp, a gentleman, a poet, a dreamer, a lonely fellow always hopeful of romance and adventure. He would have you believe he is a scientist, a musician, a duke, a polo player. However, he's not above picking up a cigarette butt or robbing a baby of its candy.' It is this myriad of diverse characteristics which made the character so popular and so widely fascinating. Perhaps the central idea was something that is often at the core of the greatest comedy: the split between what the character imagines himself to be and what he actually is; and the split between what he desires of life and what society will permit him to have.

His popularity was unprecedented. It was not long before he was receiving literally millions of fan letters a year. When he came to England in 1921 he received 73,000 letters from London alone. Part of the popularity was simply the brilliance of his comedy technique – his breathtaking skills at mime, his extraordinary physical agility and control, even in tiny details (like that moment in a 1916 short, *The Count*, where he is doing the splits in a dance but manages to pull himself upright by hooking his cane to a chandelier). But what set him apart was the human dimension of the character – the dignity (his derby), the vanity (his moustache), the dash (his coat and cane), and the air of shabby gentility. In his morning promenade in *The Kid*, he enters with a sardine tin as a cigarette case and with gloves that are more hole than glove, and then proceeds to demonstrate the art of comic counterpoint, as he sets up a tension between his tatty garments and his finicky gestures and shows us a vagabond with the mannerisms of an aristocrat. On the one hand, the joke is on snobs and on people who put on pretentious airs. But on a deeper level it is a character portrait of a man who, however absurdly, is clinging to the last vestiges of his dignity as tightly as he is clinging to his collapsing trousers; someone who is making the best of his appalling situation.

Remembering that many of his early audiences in America must have been made up of immigrants living in squalid houses and suffering from dreadful malnutrition, one is not surprised that the Tramp was such a hero and tonic. His concerns (such as where the next meal was coming from) were often their concerns. They could identify with him and probably feel the emotional authenticity of Chaplin's performance, for whom the Tramp's clothes were more than a comic costume but a remembrance of things past and perhaps even a reminder of a kind of life that his comic genius might have saved him from. The Tramp's comedy made them laugh, which might in turn have made their own situation a little easier to bear, for in laughter mankind distances itself momentarily from its faults and its frailties. More than that, he gave them hope, for the Tramp was a little David against the Goliath of society.

BELOW: Chaplin in pensive mood as he sizes up the situation in *The Kid*.

Chaplin's rise to popularity occurred with astonishing suddenness. While at Mack Sennett's Keystone Company in 1914, he had done some traditional comic roles (appearing in female disguise in *The Masquerader*), but also began to direct one-reelers which gave him more freedom to develop his own style and character. As a measure of his increasing fame, the Essanay Company in 1915 felt obliged to offer him as much as $1250 a week to tempt him away. (Only two years later, First National Films were to pay him a cool one million dollars, a recognition that by that time he was the most popular man in the world.) It was at Essanay that Chaplin began his professional association with the actress Edna Purviance, who was to appear alongside Chaplin in over 30 movies, and with the cameraman Rollie Totheroh, who was to be his regular cinematographer for the next 30 years, up to *Monsieur Verdoux*.

Of the 15 films Chaplin made during the year for Essanay, perhaps the two most significant were *The Bank* and *The Tramp*. The former has a wish-fulfilment structure in which the Tramp dreams of being loved by a typist but is rudely awakened; and the latter ends with a famous shot, later to become a trademark, as he walks away from the camera on his own down a long road into an uncertain future. (Chaplin was to repeat that shot, with slight variations, for our very last view of the Tramp in movies at the end of *Modern Times* in 1936.)

TOP LEFT: And so to bed: Chaplin finds himself trapped in *One A.M.*

ABOVE: The watch routine in *The Pawnshop*.

LEFT: Chaplin in *The Pawnshop*.

ABOVE: Chaplin begs money off Leo White (right) in *The Vagabond*.

In contrast to the predominant slapstick style of the period, both films add an element of pathos to the comedy, something learnt from Dickens, perhaps, but something that was to be enlarged and elaborated in Chaplin and became one of his major characteristics. His sentiment, as well as his comedy, became a form of social revenge. He wanted to make society weep for having made him weep.

In 1916 he signed a one-year contract at Mutual. His price in a year had increased eightfold: he was now offered $10,000 a week. His 12 two-reelers during this period contain some of his greatest and most famous comedy. It ranges from the broad humor of *The Pawnshop* (with its famous routine where Charlie, asked to repair a watch, reduces it to little pieces) and *One A.M.* (where he does an astonishing drunk act, fighting losing battles with stuffed animals, sliding rugs, a swinging pendulum and a push-button bed), to the more serious undertones of *The Vagabond, Easy Street*, and *The Immigrant*. *The Vagabond* is a mini-drama in which Charlie, as an itinerant fiddler, gets caught up with a brutal family on the road. He falls forlornly in love with a beautiful girl (Purviance) who, however, is more attracted to a prissy artist (in retaliation, Charlie flicks a fly in his face), and who turns out to be the daughter of a rich family (Charlie shakes the hand of her rich mother and then suspiciously smells his own hand for comparison). *Easy Street* sees him as a cop in a slum district, mastering the bullies through guile more than strength, and turning a blind eye when a mother steals for her starving children. (As in *Modern Times* he argued that the crime

FAR RIGHT: A policeman watches the dishonest but ingenious practices of Tramp and Kid in *The Kid*.

LEFT: A startled Chaplin, as a prisoner on the run, gives an even more startled congregation a silent sermon on the theme of David and Goliath. From *The Pilgrim*.

there is not in the act itself but in the cause of its necessity.) As well as the famous shot of the immigrants being roped off at the very moment they see America's famous symbol of Liberty, *The Immigrant* mixes hilarious comedy with strong social commentary. This shot does seem, in retrospect, to be an ominous anticipation of Chaplin's future difficulties with America, culminating in his European exile when the US Immigration Department in 1952 refused his re-entry into America until he answered 'charges of a political nature and moral turpitude.' But at the time Chaplin was probably simply illustrating what he saw as the essential outcast nature of the Tramp, as permanent outsider and immigrant in a society to which he never belongs and which he can never accept.

In 1917 he signed for First National Films and made eight movies in five years, a sign of the greater preparation he was now demanding and also of the increasing length of the films themselves. *Shoulder Arms* (1918) was one of his most daring pictures, a comedy which was the only great film to be made about World War I at the time. As later with *The Great Dictator*, it was thought that the subject-matter might prove too difficult and tragic to be the object of comedy, but he even succeeded in

making the appalling conditions of the trenches seem hilarious, as Charlie settles down for the night only to find that he is sleeping underwater with a frog for company. In *The Pilgrim* (1923), in which he satirizes an American religious rural community, he plays an escaped convict who is compelled to impersonate a minister. It leads to some splendid comic situations, when he begins to hallucinate that the choir is actually a jury, or at the pulpit has to mime the story of David and Goliath, or,

ABOVE: 'It's dangerous at this time to make fun of the war', said Cecil B De Mille. But Chaplin did it in *Shoulder Arms*. With Sydney Chaplin (left).

at another stage, gets so distracted by a rebellious child that he ends up serving a guest's hat as a delicious pudding.

But Chaplin's greatest success of the early 1920s was *The Kid* (1921), the longest film he had made up to that time (six reels) and also the most personal, drawing on a lot of painful memories and experiences from his own life: the pain of separation from parent figures; and the fear instilled by people (welfare workers, the police) who represent the authority of society. It was also the most overtly emotional of his films up to that time, provoking tears along with laughter; and also had a strong vein of social criticism, about how society treated its unfortunates, whether they be an unmarried mother, a tramp, or a kid with no socially sanctioned parents. *The Kid* was certainly Chaplin's biggest risk up to that time and turned out to be one of his biggest successes. One might add that it was also the only Chaplin film in which he was almost upstaged by his co-star, the extraordinarily talented five-year-old, Jackie Coogan.

The film is basically about the relationship between the Tramp and a child who has been abandoned at birth and whom the Tramp has (at first relucantly) adopted. When the boy grows up he joins the Tramp in business: that is, it is the kid's job to break people's windows and the Tramp's to come along innocently afterwards to offer his services as a glazier. One suspects that Chaplin is offering this as a not very flattering metaphor for big business: in Chaplin's terms, a combination of destruction and deception. It is a vision he was to develop more murderously in his black comedy *Monsieur Verdoux*.

The Kid really hinges on two separation scenes. The first is the scene when the welfare authorities come to take the kid away from the Tramp and put him in the workhouse, throwing the kid into the truck as if he is an animal being taken to the slaughterhouse. What follows is one of the most extraordinary chase scenes of silent comedy, as the Tramp eludes the police over the rooftops while still keeping the truck in his sights. The ingenious thing about it is not simply that it is different from the usual car chase (a car pursued by someone on foot over rooftops) but that the tone is so different: the accent is not on

slapstick and comedy but sentiment and suspense. When the Tramp rescues the kid, they are both genuinely crying, which, Coogan was to recall, 'was a shock to the audience . . . to see this great clown, this mischievous tramp, really crying.'

The second separation occurs when the kid has been reclaimed by his real mother, and the Tramp, having searched for the boy in vain, collapses on a step and falls asleep. What follows is one of Chaplin's strangest dream sequences where the Tramp, at a moment of extreme crisis and despair, has a vision of Heaven, which is not without its comic overtones (the Tramp has angelic wings, but they itch) nor without its darker side, when sin creeps in. It is a scene of appropriate simplicity, but it reflects the Tramp as a dreamer and the way he can sometimes rise above his awful situation through sheer effort of imagination. (He also does this in *The Gold Rush* (1925) by making a meal of boots and laces seem like a gourmet's paradise.) The dream scene also prepares us for the fairytale finale in which Tramp and kid are reunited: might this too be a dream?

The Kid has some wonderful comic

moments, particularly when the Tramp is playing 'mother' to his new charge, and having to find a new use for familiar objects. But there is always an underlying harshness. Chaplin's criticism is wide-ranging: of the social attitude to the unmarried mother, which impels her to abandon a baby she loves; and of the pompous behavior of the police and welfare administrators to people it assumes are basically garbage. There is a chilling image of human avarice also in that moment when a fly settles greedily on the paper of the proprietor of the boarding-house where Tramp and kid are staying, as he reads hungrily of the reward out for the kid. Comedy will win out, but only just.

The films were growing more ambitious not only thematically but also structurally: Chaplin was now ready to expand his ideas to feature length. His three features during the 1920s contain two brilliant eccentricities and one unqualified masterpiece. The eccentricities were *A Woman of Paris* (1923) and *The Circus* (1928); the masterpiece was *The Gold Rush*.

A Woman of Paris is eccentric, partly because Chaplin himself did not appear

RIGHT: Chaplin and Jackie Coogan in *The Kid.*

LEFT: Adolph Menjou and Edna Purviance in *A Woman of Paris.*

apart from a brief walk-on as a railway porter, and partly because of its serious theme. It is a sophisticated moral tragedy of the corruption of a young country girl (Edna Purviance) who, jilted by her fiancé, travels to Paris and is seduced by a suave playboy (Adolphe Menjou). For its time the film was quite outspoken in its sexual frankness, and subtle in its social comedy, as in the famous scene when the socialite heroine petulantly throws her jewelry out

of the window and then has to rush down and reclaim it from a bemused drunk who momentarily cannot believe his luck. The ending is particularly ironic and harsh, with the playboy passing the girl in the country without seeing her and, in a final conversation with a friend, seeming barely able to remember her. Hailed as a milestone in film art by Chaplin's fellow directors (Ernst Lubitsch, Sergei Eisenstein, Michael Powell were only some who pro-

ABOVE, TOP RIGHT AND RIGHT: Chaplin in danger, in love (with Merna Kennedy), and in practice in *The Circus*.

fessed to be bowled over by the film), *A Woman of Paris* was not a popular success. As with Woody Allen in our own day when he shifted to straight drama, audiences resisted the change of direction, yearning for the style of the earlier, funnier films. The film was withdrawn and remained virtually unseen until, shortly before his death, Chaplin sanctioned its re-issue and composed a new music score.

The Circus is a Chaplin eccentricity only in the sense that it is one of the least well-known of his feature comedies and that Chaplin does not even mention it in his own autobiography, despite the fact that he was awarded a Special Oscar for his acting, writing, and directing of it. (Chaplin's only other Oscar came for his score for *Limelight* awarded 20 years after the film was made because it had been boycotted by distributors in America on its first release.) It is a somewhat patchy film, though with many flashes of comic invention. The opening is particularly lively. The antics of a pickpocket lead to a chase; there is a confrontation in a hall of mirrors; then there is an attempt by the Tramp to pass himself off as a clockwork model. This is followed by a situation where, in trying to escape the police, Chaplin inadvertently takes over the circus performance, is funnier than the resident clowns, and is therefore offered a job. Two scenes represent some of the funniest comedy in the film: the first where Charlie, attempting to walk the tightrope,

is suddenly assailed by escaping monkeys; the second where he finds himself locked in a cage with a sleeping lion (when a dog suddenly barks, the Tramp puts his fingers into his *own* ears, as if that will eliminate the danger). The film's final image, though, is forlorn even by Chaplin's standards. After failing to win the girl he loves, he sits alone amid the debris as the circus troupe pulls out, then trudges off into the distance. He has rarely looked more isolated or more (to quote James Joyce) like 'an outcast at life's feast.'

If *The Circus* was never a favorite film of Chaplin's, *The Gold Rush*, by contrast, was an instant classic and was the film Chaplin said he would most like to be remembered by. He called it 'A Dramatic Comedy,' for the film was actually inspired by an incident of cannibalism that took place while

men were prospecting for gold. Chaplin shot on the actual location where the incident had taken place. Hardly surprising, then, that hunger is a pervasive theme in the film as the Tramp, prospecting for gold in the Klondike, is beset by misfortune and danger and at one stage mistaken for a chicken by a hunger-crazed miner. Food is at the center of the movie's two most famous set-pieces: the dance of the rolls, as the Tramp improvizes with some food as he waits in vain for the heroine (Georgia Hale) to appear; and the meal of the boots, which he boils in a pot, then separates the nail-studded sole from the tender top before settling down for the meal, twirling the shoelaces on his fork like spaghetti, and sucking the nails like chicken bones. Hunger has either driven him mad, or it is a truly heroic instance of the Tramp's dogged

determination to find something sustaining out of something awful – to find, in a way, some tenderness behind the toughness of life. Charlie looks especially vulnerable in *The Gold Rush*, often memorably framed on his own against a bleak wintry setting, with only a thin shawl as his defense against the cold. Nowhere did the Tramp's solitude seem so vast nor his resilience so gallant. If *The Gold Rush* has a special place in Chaplin's affections and in those of his devotees, the reason is that he never contrived a better image of humanity under the most extreme conditions, which made comedy in those circumstances all the more powerful, precious, and poignant.

It is something of a convention to say that Chaplin only got into trouble when he opened his mouth – in life, as in films. On the silent screen he reigned supreme; the

talkies spelt trouble. It is true that Chaplin loathed the idea of the talkies and for a long time turned his back on them, still using titles in *City Lights* (1931) and *Modern Times* (1936) and allowing the Tramp only one vocal performance – a nonsense song in *Modern Times* – before his final exit from the screen. But the change that came over Chaplin had more to it than just a difficult readjustment to developing cinema technology. The world was changing too, and not for the better. The contemporary issues now confronting Chaplin were no longer only injustice, hunger, unemployment, and poverty, but evil, persecution, and mass murder on a hitherto unthinkable scale. It was a depersonalized and demoralized world in which the humanity of the Tramp had no place, which was the reason that, at the end of *Modern Times*, he

ABOVE: Mack Swain, Chaplin and dog in *The Gold Rush*.

ABOVE: Chaplin saves a drunken millionaire (Harry Myers) from drowning in *City Lights* after the millionaire had attempted suicide.

RIGHT: Chaplin and Virginia Cherril in *City Lights*.

finally disappeared down the road, never to return.

Yet it was a world which Chaplin as an artist was determined to confront. It is a measure of his greatness that the films he made in the sound era still provoke intense critical argument and anger. Did they represent a sad falling-off of his creative powers and a betrayal of his comic talent, or did they reveal an even more profound insight into society and character and an even greater subtlety of artistic form and symbolism? For the record, let it be said that this writer believes the latter, and that the films he made between 1931 and 1952 are the crowning glories of his career and among the supreme works of art of the twentieth century.

Reputed to be Woody Allen's favorite screen comedy, *City Lights* (1931) was Chaplin's eagerly awaited first film of the sound era. It eschewed dialogue but it did make comic use of sound, as in the moment when Charlie swallows a toy whistle at a rich man's party and his subsequent hiccoughs not only disrupt a musical performance but also inadvertently summon all the dogs of the neighboring district. The humor resides mainly in Chaplin's familiar physical dexterity, never more impressive than in the scene when he does a soft-shoe shuffle to evade a boxer whom he is fighting to raise money.

Nevertheless the central situation of the film is intensely dramatic and one of Chaplin's most ingeniously contrived. The Tramp has saved a drunken millionaire (Harry Myers) from drowning. When drunk, the millionaire treats Charlie like a king, showering him with money which Charlie donates toward an eye operation for a blind flower-seller (Virginia Cherrill) that could restore her sight. When sober, the millionaire treats the Tramp as an objectionable parasite and finally wrongfully accuses him of theft and has him sent to prison.

The film is about different kinds of blindness. Because she cannot see his shabby appearance, the flower-girl is not prejudiced against the Tramp but nevertheless still assumes his generosity betokens wealth and breeding. What irritates the millionaire (when sober) about the Tramp is that he probably recognizes in Charlie an independent spirit, a side of himself he has

driven out in order to become materially successful.

Everything evolves toward the unforgettable last scene when the Tramp comes out of prison and passes the flower shop which the girl, her sight restored, now owns. Patronizingly she offers this poor tramp a flower and it is only when their fingers touch that she realizes (like Pip's recognition of the convict in Dickens's *Great Expectations*) the identity of her benefactor. At which point Chaplin constructs one of the greatest close-ups in the history of the cinema, which is of the Tramp's face at this point of recognition – apologetic, delighted that she can see, but unnervingly, through her reaction, seeing himself for the first time.

Chaplin's last non-talking film, and his last to feature the Tramp, was *Modern Times* (1936). Explaining the impulse behind the film, Chaplin said: 'I wanted to say something about the way life is being standardized and channelized, and men turned into machines.' Some ungrateful critics thought the movie almost a copy of René Clair's satirical film on a similar theme, *A Nous la*

ABOVE: The final close-up of *City Lights* when the Tramp confronts the flower girl – and himself.

ABOVE: Chaplin gets ready for his boxing match in *City Lights*.

FAR RIGHT: A cog in the machine: Chaplin in *Modern Times*.

Liberté (1931), though Clair himself commented benignly that 'I would be honored beyond measure if a genius like Chaplin thought any of my ideas worth stealing.'

The mechanization of man forms the basis of most of the humor of the first part of the film. The Tramp's job of tightening nuts on an assembly line is so repetitive that he is still twitching when the machine stops, and he later mistakes the buttons on a secretary's dress for the nuts of the machine. Used as a guinea-pig for a feeding machine that has been designed to eliminate the lunch-hour, Charlie is attacked by his food when the machine gets out of control. A lot of key themes are being introduced here: hunger, the repetitive circularity of assembly-line existence, the regimentation of the masses, and the depersonalization of the individual. When Charlie falls into the machinery and in a sense becomes part of its mechanism, the experience will precipitate his nervous breakdown.

At this point the film broadens its perspective to evoke life in Depression America, and the Tramp becomes involved with a gamine (Paulette Goddard), a child of the waterfront who has to look after her little sisters after her unemployed father has been shot dead by the police on a hunger march. There are some funny routines, when Charlie inadvertently finds himself leading a Communist parade (a somewhat ominous foretaste of the political accusations to come in his public life) or when he foils a prison escape quite by accident, being under the influence of drugs at the time. But the evocation of the times is also poignantly real: brutality, strikes, unemployment, imprisonment, and bureaucratic impersonality. At one stage Charlie prefers to stay in prison than face the world outside. Getting a job as a night watchman

34

ABOVE: Possibilities of
parole, perhaps: Chaplin
and the chaplain's wife
(Myra McKinney) in
Modern Times.

in a department store, Charlie disturbs
some robbers and recognizes one of them
as a friend from prison. 'We ain't burglars,'
the friend says, 'we're hungry.' In one of
his funniest routines, Charlie skates blind-
fold in the deserted department store
toward an unsuspected abyss. It is a mirac-
ulous piece of graceful physical comedy,
but its undertones are somewhat disturbing: perhaps a reflection of Chaplin's vision
of man's journey through life.

On one level *Modern Times* merely con-
tinues what Chaplin's comedy had always
been about: the search for life's basics –
food, love, and money (generally in that
order). To this end, at one point he has to
wait on tables and sing. When his cuff, on
which the song lyrics have been written,
flies off with his elaborate opening flourish, he has to improvise a garbled nonsense
song to earn his keep: the Tramp's first and
only words on film and a brilliant routine.

But there is also something different about
Modern Times. The Tramp's dreams of domesticity – an actual cow rather than a milkman at the door, an impossibly large steak
– are exaggerated as always for comic effect
but also exaggerated now to indicate their
unreality. Accommodation and assimila-
tion are no longer possible or even desir-
able for the Tramp in these modern times.
His enemy now is faceless, soul-less, in-
human, robotic.

There were complaints about Chaplin's
continued disdain for talkies and his use of
titles, and some thought his view of
modern society old-fashioned and
romantically pessimistic. It was a familiar
argument, also used against Dickens on
novels like *Hard Times* and *Little Dorrit*,
neglecting to note that these artists were
talking about universal themes and ten-
dencies rather than specific historical
events. The potential horrors of deperson-

LEFT: Tangled up with the machinery in *Modern Times*.

alization and the desensitizing of the individual in an oppressively technological age are still with us, perhaps more so. The Tramp's attempted solution to being terrorized by a system is hardly a profound political program, but nor is it hopelessly out-of-date. Indeed one could argue that it anticipated the activities of the 1960s dropouts: find a suitable mate and opt out of society altogether, with its spoonfeeding of mechanized responses. The Tramp walks off down the road with the gamine at the end of *Modern Times*, never to return: the last hobo perhaps, or the first hippy, but certainly as James Agee called him, the most human of all screen clowns and 'as centrally representative of humanity, as many-sided and mysterious, as Hamlet.'

BELOW: The Tramp's farewell: Chaplin walks away down the road with Paulette Goddard at the end of *Modern Times*.

When François Truffaut reviewed *The Great Dictator* (1940) on its reissue in 1957, he made a comment that should be engraved on the skull of every Chaplin detractor: 'I despise the set mind that rejects ambitious work from someone who's supposed to be a comic. . . . If Chaplin has been told that he is a poet or a philosopher, it's because it's true and he was right to believe what he heard. Without willing it or knowing it, Chaplin helped men live; later, when he became aware of it, would it not have been criminal to stop trying to help them even more?' Even today, it is possible to underestimate the risk Chaplin was taking in making *The Great Dictator*: an anti-Fascist satire at a time when American foreign policy was still isolationist and neutral; a comedy which, if it had failed, could have seemed unpardonably distasteful. For in it Chaplin was to exploit one of the most bizarre resemblances in modern history: the physical resemblance between himself and Adolf Hitler. The French critic André Bazin called it a settling of accounts, Chaplin's revenge against Hitler's double crime of elevating himself to the level of the gods and stealing Charlie's mustache. The film is a funny but also ferocious attack on totalitarianism and the cult of the Great Leader. As Ernst Lubitsch was later to do in *To Be or Not to Be* (1942), surely influenced by Chaplin's example, he holds Nazism up to ridicule in the hope that the corresponding laughter will make it impossible for such a political philosophy ever to be taken seriously.

The main plot twist derives from Chaplin's playing of two roles: a meek Jewish barber, who has obvious affinities with the characterization of the Tramp; and the dictator of Tomania, Adenoid Hynkel. There are also fine performances by Paulette Goddard as the barber's girlfriend Hannah; Henry Daniell as Hynkel's advisor; and Jack Oakie as an uproariously funny version of Mussolini, here called Benzino Napolini, dictator of Bacteria. The most memorable routines, though, are Chaplin's: as the barber, rhythmically shaving a customer to the strains of Brahms's Hungarian Dance during the 'Happy Hour' permitted by the State; or, as Hynkel, performing the extraordinary ballet with the globe, as the dictator is likened to an air-filled balloon afloat on a bubble of pure megalomania. Everything comes together in the moment when the Jewish barber is mistaken for the dictator and is asked to make a speech setting out his beliefs. What follows from Chaplin, after a career of silence, is an avalanche of words, a point in his career from which there is no turning back, and an explicit spelling out of what the deepest feelings in his films have meant.

Some find this final speech over-explicit,

rhetorical, and sentimental. But it is beautifully prepared for in the context of the film,
triggered by the word 'hope' and a verbal
torrent that attempts to turn back the tide
of history. It is enormously courageous at
this historical moment, refusing to take the
line of political compromise and daring to
spell out the danger that was looming for
the free world: 'Greed has poisoned men's
souls – has barricaded the world with hate
– has goose-stepped us into misery and
bloodshed. . . . More than machinery we
need humanity. More than cleverness, we
need kindness and gentleness.' Finally, it
is the decisive turning-point in Chaplin's
career, when he drops the Tramp's persona once and for all and, because the
situation is so serious that he can no longer
remain silent, speaks to us in his own
voice. No one sensitive to the music of
Chaplin's cinematic language could fail to
be moved by the audaciousness behind the

concept and form of *The Great Dictator*, by
the anger behind the laughter, and the
laughter behind the anger. That lover of
decency, democracy and direct, uncor-
rupted language, George Orwell, said of it
that, 'the allure of power politics will be a
fraction weaker for every human being
who sees this film.'

One of the saddest moments in all Chaplin is a scene on a rooftop in *The Great Dictator* when the Jewish barber is watching his
house burn down. Although he is being
offered words of comfort by Hannah, we,
like him, are not listening to the words but
looking at the devastation. A master of
movement, Chaplin here makes use of the
most eloquent stillness: as Jean-Louis Bar-
rault commented, his immobility here is a
perfect 'mime of despair,' reflecting 'the
choreography of anguish.' Chaplin's pro-
phecy of holocaust was not to be heeded
and, because he had chosen to attack Hitler

three years before the United States entered the war, he was later to be attacked for what was peculiarly called 'premature anti-fascism.'

Indeed the 1940s were to be a particularly traumatic decade for Chaplin. His personal relationships for a long time had aroused a certain amount of public disquiet. Perhaps because they reminded him of a childish innocence he had never known, Chaplin had always been attracted to younger women. All his first three wives were under the age of twenty when they married him. The second, Lita Grey, appropriately played the child-vamp in the dream sequence of *The Kid*, and the third was Paulette Goddard who remarked of Chaplin that, 'at least he never brought his work home with him. He was the most humorless man I ever met.' Public disapproval of his private life flared up when he became the subject of a paternity suit instigated by an actress, Joan Barry. Chaplin was found innocent of any immorality but, in spite of overwhelming medical evidence to the contrary, was still adjudged to be the father of the child. In 1943 the 54-year-old Chaplin had married the 18-year-old Oona O'Neill, daughter of the distinguished American playwright Eugene O'Neill who strongly disapproved of the match (which turned out to be blissfully happy). But if his personal life attracted criticism at this time, his socialist and pacifist political views provoked a storm of hostility. He could hardly have chosen a worse moment to bring out *Monsieur Verdoux* (1947), a film whose bitter, anti-war tone was quite in conflict with the mood of an America engaged in a Cold War against the Soviet Union and insisting on patriotism from its film-makers.

Based on an idea by Orson Welles (who always claimed to have foreseen and predicted Oona O'Neill's marriage to Chaplin before they had met when he read her palm during his magic act), *Monsieur Verdoux* (1947) is a black comedy of murder. Verdoux is a French bank-teller who has lost his savings in the Depression which has imperiled his support of his invalid wife and little boy. His solution is to hit on a scheme of courting and marrying rich women and then murdering them for their money. He speculates; and then makes a killing. Murder seems to him to be a logical extension of business and, like a business-

man, it takes him all over France, so that he seldom sees his family. 'Wars, conflicts – it's all business,' he will tell a journalist toward the end while in his death-cell awaiting execution. 'One murder makes a villain; millions a hero. Numbers sanctify.'

The film's seeming equation between the ethics of cut-throat capitalism and murder would certainly not have endeared him to the postwar American Establishment. But, in fact, the argument of the film cannot be so grossly simplified as that. In a sense, Verdoux is a symbol of the classic dilemma of a country at war: in the defense of hearth and home, are not desperate, unethical, even murderous strategies justified? (Chaplin would say not, but his characterization of Verdoux raises the question in a particularly urgent form). And if the film takes its critique of the depersonalization of capitalism even further than it did in *Modern Times*, one should note that, as a

ABOVE: Verdoux and one of his victims: Chaplin and Margaret Hoffman in *Monsieur Verdoux*.

ABOVE: Chaplin as
Monsieur Verdoux.

what might have happened if the Tramp, instead of turning the other cheek to social injustice, had survived it, accepted it, and suddenly and malevolently struck back. Verdoux is the Tramp turned inside out: rich not poor, dapper not shabby, embittered not hopeful, misogynistic not romantic, murderous not merciful.

In the light of all this, it might seem surprising that the film is also funny. Yet Chaplin is splendid in the moments of slapstick, as, for example, when he thinks he has inadvertently poisoned himself, or when he fails to drown the most raucous of his wives. Even our introduction to the character is a masterly miniature of comic incongruity: Verdoux in his garden, prissily cutting roses and rescuing a caterpillar, while at the same time a cloud of black smoke gathers behind him – implicitly, the incinerated remains of his late, latest wife. (It was a visual joke emulated in another great black comedy of murder, Robert Hamer's 1949 Ealing comedy, *Kind Hearts and Coronets*, but it is an image that has also deliberately chilling overtones of the gas chambers, the Holocaust.) There is a hilarious long shot of the murder boat, comically small on the lake, as if already anticipating the failure of Verdoux's attempt. Even the recurrent shots of the train wheels as Verdoux goes from one victim to the next has its part to play: a kind of visual catchphrase that winds up the film for its next phase, but also perhaps suggesting not only the character's thrashing energy but his increasing mechanization.

There are some superb supporting performances, particularly from Martha Raye as the most monstrously indestructible of Verdoux's wives, and from Marilyn Nash as a friendless woman whom Verdoux has picked up in order to test a traceless poison on her, but who is spared when she discloses that she would 'kill for love.' Chaplin's own performance is perhaps his finest ever and one of the greatest on film. Verdoux is his most complex creation, a mixture of good and evil, intelligence and coldness, and Chaplin explores every nuance, from what the critic Louis Giannetti has called the 'mincing effeminacy' of the beginning to the 'tragic grandeur' of the end, where he is as alienated and serene as Camus's Outsider. 'May the Lord have mercy on your soul,' says the priest to him,

counterbalance to that, the characterization of Verdoux is more deeply critical even than that of the drunken millionaire in *City Lights*; both are men for whom the pursuit of money has robbed them of their humanity. Verdoux kills for love but, in so doing, becomes ever more estranged from the family he adores and from his own personality.

There is a terrifying postwar logic to the film, as Chaplin the supreme humanist surveys a world that has in a way gone mad and committed horrors on a hitherto unprecedented scale. *The Great Dictator* tried to reverse the tide of history through ridicule; *Monsieur Verdoux* looks it straight in the eye. It is a film in which something snaps in Chaplin. He contemplates the proposition that the insanity and injustice of the world might finally overwhelm even a decent man and turn him into a monster. Verdoux is the shadow side of the Tramp,

ABOVE: Chaplin as Calvero, Claire Bloom as Terry in *Limelight*.

to which he replies: 'Why not? It belongs to him.' They are setting off from his cell for his execution, when Verdoux turns back. 'I have never tasted rum,' he says, sipping the drink on his table, his last taste of life. The final shot as he walks away from the camera towards an all-too-certain future is spine-chilling: as if the Tramp were heading for the guillotine.

'These are desperate days . . .' Verdoux says at one stage. 'When the world looks grim and dark, I think of another world.' After the vituperation leveled at *Monsieur Verdoux*, which Chaplin thought one of his most important works, and the vilification leveled at his moral character and his political beliefs, it is not surprising that Chaplin was now tempted to take stock and look back. His final American film, *Limelight* (1952), is a kind of testament. Set in the London of 1914, it is an evocation of the artist's past. Dealing with the love relation-

ship between a young ballerina (Claire Bloom) and an ageing clown old enough to be her father, Chaplin is surely working out some of the anxieties he must have felt in the early stages of his own marriage to Oona. Above all, in his telling of the story of the clown Calvero deserted by his audience, but who has one last triumph before dying, significantly, on stage, Chaplin is in a sense saying his own farewell to his audience. He was to make two more films, *A King in New York* (1957) and *The Countess from Hong Kong* (1966) but these were to be footnotes to a career. *Limelight* is really his final statement.

Couched as a kind of farewell to music-hall and its traditions, which had nurtured Chaplin's talent, it is equally a farewell to silent comedy. In his final stage appearance, Calvero will have a partner, and, for the first and only time in their careers, Chaplin will share a dressing room with

Buster Keaton. Their comedy sketch together – Chaplin as a left-handed violinist who somehow contrives to fall into the orchestra pit, Keaton as a short-sighted pianist whose sheets of music keep sliding on to the keys and who inadvertently puts his foot through Calvero's violin – is undoubtedly the comic highlight of the film. Yet it is arguable that this sketch is as much moving as it is funny. This is the ambiguity of Calvero's final triumph: is the audience applauding the performance or the memory? Is their delight admiration or nostalgia?

As a clown down on his luck, Calvero saves a ballerina from suicide and, at the time of his own greatest despair, she rediscovers a new impulse to live. Age will give way to youth and, as with *The Great Dictator*, Chaplin's final images are not of himself but of the face and form of a young

LEFT: Calvero's comeback: Claire Bloom and Chaplin in *Limelight*. 'I thought you hated the theater,' she says. 'I do,' he replies. 'I also hate the sight of blood – but it's in my veins.'

woman who seems to carry the hope of the future. At the same time, just as Calvero stubbornly refuses to adapt his act to the times, so Chaplin keeps to the world and the style that he knows, creating a film that is somehow outside time. In the face of everything – changing times, tastes, and techniques – he will stick to his dated but ageless routines, insisting that he can still make them work. There is a wonderful moment when Calvero is preparing for his final performance and tells the ballerina that 'this is where I belong.' 'I thought you hated the theater,' she says, to which he replies: 'I do. I also hate the sight of blood, but it's in my veins.' The compulsion of artistic creativity, even when uninspired or undesired or unappreciated, has never been better defined.

Chaplin's final two films were something of an anti-climax, though not without

the king has a face-lift which makes him look like a grotesque and which anyway starts to come apart when he begins to laugh. The more serious side of the film is its evocation of the McCarthy era in America and the atmosphere of persecution, particularly revealed when the young son of an American Communist is forced to 'name names' to save his parents from prison. (The part is sensitively played by Chaplin's own son Michael). The motif of spying – whether through keyholes or through hidden cameras – is a consistent one in the film. The contagion of fear and paranoia is powerfully conveyed, but the film is less bitter than it is often painted, and shot through with an engaging self-satire directed at Chaplin's reputed meanness, vanity, and weakness for younger women. There is serenity beneath the savage satire.

LEFT: Send in the clowns: Buster Keaton and Chaplin share a dressing-room in *Limelight*.

their points of interest. In *A King in New York* (1957), he plays an exiled king, who, having aimed for Utopia, has been deposed by revolution, and is now an old man forced to adjust to a new, alien world. Chaplin has some very funny digs at American TV commercials, notably when the king almost chokes on a whisky whose delights he has just been praising; and a quietly amusing satire on the American obsession with youth in a sequence when

In *The Countess from Hong Kong* (1966), for the first time since *A Woman of Paris* over forty years before, Chaplin directed, but did not star in, a story of a refugee's attempts to attain American citizenship. The stars are Sophia Loren as the refugee and Marlon Brando as a disgruntled American ambassador. There are some sharp comic sallies at the world of wealth and international politics, but mainly the film is a somewhat stolid shipboard farce, enlivened by the

ABOVE: King Shahdov (Chaplin) uses his hostess (Joan Ingram) and some cutlery to illustrate the horror of being in the dentist's chair when the dentist has to take a phone call. From *A King in New York*.

charm of the two stars, and by choice cameos from Margaret Rutherford, who at one stage mistakenly believes she is being serenaded as a raving beauty, and Tippi Hedren as the ambassador's astringent wife. Patrick Cargill's performance as Brando's manservant almost steals the film, particularly in a marvelously played scene with Brando where master informs servant that he has decided that the latter should be married in about ten minutes' time. Perhaps predictably, Brando found Chaplin's working methods, in which he demonstrated what he wanted from the

BELOW: The King flirts with Ann (Dawn Addams) in *A King in New York*.

actor and then the actor had to imitate it exactly, quite uncongenial. Jackie Coogan commented on *The Kid* that Chaplin would 'explain to me *what* he wanted to do, and then explain *why* he wanted me to do it, because he believed that in comedy the mechanics induced the emotion.' This, of course, is the reverse of 'the Method' style of acting, which believes that motivation induces the action and not vice-versa, so it is not surprising that relations between Brando and Chaplin were so strained.

The problem for Chaplin as a director of actors was, as Coogan said, that 'he could

do anything . . . he could do it better than the guy who originated it.' There probably has never been a greater all-round talent than Chaplin's in the movies, who not only acted, but also directed and wrote the music as well as the script, which in certain cases – 'Smile' from *Modern Times*, the theme from *Limelight*, 'This is my Song' from *The Countess from Hong Kong* – became hugely popular. How to summarize and encompass the magnitude of this talent?

Chaplin's mastery of the art of physical comedy was complete. His body was an extraordinarily supple and subtle comic instrument. He could skate, dance, juggle, walk a tightrope: not just adeptly but expertly. When running to escape a pursuer, he had a trick of hopping and skidding on one leg while, with the other, he would round a corner. He could fall and somersault with a cup of tea in his hand – the so-called 'tea-cup roll' – and still emerge without a drop being spilt. He could mime anything in existence, standing in for a tree when he is hiding from the enemy in *Shoulder Arms* and, for the benefit of the downcast ballerina in *Limelight*,

imitating in turn, and with breathtaking skill, a rock, a rose, a Japanese tree, and a pansy, first sad then gay. His hands alone converse in *A Dog's Life* while the rest of his body is hidden, and they act out a ballet of anguish and self-pity in *Limelight* as he tells of his humiliating return to the stage.

If his body was the most expressive of comic objects, he was also the most inventive user of objects for comic effect. There is generally a double comedy at work here, where the object either resists being used for the purpose intended or the actor adapts it for a more immediate use. As an example of the first, one thinks of the recalcitrant bed in *One A.M.*, which obstinately refuses to stay put as the drunk tries to turn in for the night. As an example of the latter, one might think of the Tramp's ingenious use of a street lamp in *Easy Street* to anesthetize then asphyxiate the neighborhood bully. The whole opening of *Modern Times* is a satire of mechanized movement, though as the machine becomes ascendant over man, it becomes less easy to be funny in this way, for humor requires a soul.

All of his gifts were synthesized in the creation of the Tramp. The character was physically funny, with his duck-like walk, his trapezoid mustache, his absurdly baggy trousers, his twirling cane. But it was the personality that appealed: his charm and cheek, his brazen cheating, his quick-wittedness and his quick-footed agility, and his ability, in particular, to get the better of the big and the bully. He cut people down to size, particularly the rich and the self-righteous, the pompous and the powerful. By developing and expanding this personality through a wide range of situations and adventures whereby he could become cook, preacher, boxer, waiter, political leader, prospector, paper-hanger, mechanic, and glazier, Chaplin turned the character into a truly mythical figure. George Orwell would argue that it derived from the most basic folk-tale of the English-speaking people: Jack the Giant Killer, the little man versus the big man. If the myth gains poignancy in Chaplin's case, the reason is that it also seems applicable to his life: someone who at the outset seemed to face insurmountable odds and yet who triumphed above such immense adversity to become the most famous man in the world.

There are areas of his achievement that will always remain controversial: his pathos, his politics, which for some are a corruption of his talent. But Chaplin always saw himself as as much a crusader as a comic, not so much a troubadour as a truth-teller and, as George Bernard Shaw once remarked: 'If you want to tell people the truth, you'd better make them laugh, or they'll kill you.' Take the superb opening of *City Lights*, where a monument is pompously unveiled, only to reveal the Tramp sleeping at its foot. It is a many-layered joke, in its iconoclasm perhaps even anticipating Chaplin's own fall from the pedestal of public acclaim. What it is, above all, though, is a reminder of the poor whom we will always have with us and whom, even at the height of his fame, Chaplin obstinately refused to forget.

Chaplin died on Christmas Day, 1977. Jean Renoir said of him that he 'took note of the egotism and absurdity of the world and, like the early Christians, meekly accepts it. It is an acceptance that softens the public heart and turns it away from violent solutions.' Artistically, Chaplin was the best friend of the down-trodden, the persecuted, the underdog, since Charles Dickens. He became not only film comedy's greatest clown but its social conscience. He was the bravest, most humane of humorists, slapstick's saint whose films stand as a unique, central commentary on our century.

BELOW: Charlie Chaplin in *The Pilgrim*.

CHAPTER TWO

Buster Keaton

'With Keaton on the screen, other faces, other gestures were apt to fade: even the greatest performers were diminished. In the famous duet in *Limelight* it was Keaton struggling with the vagabond sheets of music whom one watched, not Chaplin.' This comment, by the *doyenne* of British film critics, Dilys Powell, is oddly prophetic. It anticipated the way that, after his death in 1966, Keaton's reputation was progressively to upstage that of Chaplin. Indeed nowadays it is perhaps more common to regard Keaton as Chaplin's equal, if not superior, certainly as a director, even as an actor. In part, this is simply the expression of a preference for one kind of art over another – for stoicism over sentiment, for perfection of physicality over the poeticizing of poverty. They both had genius: what is fascinating is that it was genius of a completely different kind.

Can one say that Keaton was really a better actor than Chaplin? It is hard to imagine his even attempting to scale the tragic heights of Chaplin's Monsieur Verdoux or the moving self-criticism of Chaplin's Calvero in *Limelight*. Yet there is a sense in which Keaton is one of the most extraordinary actors of the silent screen. Nothing is more misleading than the nickname of 'The Great Stoneface' for no face on film has been more eloquently expressive. 'We can see him thinking,' said the French critic Robert Benayoun, and the British film historian David Robinson went further, saying that behind those 'great melancholy unsmiling eyes . . . there is a soul.' What did this deadpan face express? James Agee has listed the qualities better than anyone: 'a one-track mind near the track's end of pure insanity; mulish imperturbality under the wildest of circumstances; an awe-inspiring sort of patience and power to endure, proper to granite but uncanny in flesh and blood. . . . When he moved his eyes it was like seeing them move in a statue.'

Can one say that Keaton was a better director than Chaplin? It is something of a critical cliché nowadays to denigrate Chaplin's direction and to dismiss his films as being of little visual interest. This is grossly unfair to someone who used the close-up

so powerfully; who could use the long shot for the most refined visual comedy (as in the attempted murder scene of *Monsieur Verdoux*); and whose mastery extended from the magical dissolve back from dream to reality in *The Kid*, to an unobtrusive but beautifully judged cut from close-up to medium shot in *Limelight* to reflect Calvero's sudden resignation and conceding of a point in a tense argument. Yet it would be true to say that, for Chaplin, form was always secondary to content. Character, situation, and theme were the primary things in Chaplin, and the camera was simply, as it were, a recording machine rather than an artistic collaborator. For Keaton it was the other way round. Content was often secondary to form, and Keaton was fascinated with the mechanics of the camera. For Chaplin the film frame essentially preserved the function of the theatrical proscenium arch: his films tended to be theatrical in form, studio-bound, consciously artificial. By contrast, location and landscape were much more important in Keaton, as were his interests in cinematic illusion and special effects.

ABOVE: Buster Keaton and Florence Turner in *College*.

RIGHT: That face: Buster Keaton.

50

Chaplin tended always to the real: Keaton sometimes to the surreal.

One might follow the implications of this a little further. Chaplin's primary interest was in the human, Keaton's in the mechanical. Chaplin's hero was opposed by society: Keaton's more often opposed by nature. Chaplin's persona was implicitly socialist, Keaton's fatalist. Chaplin's hero was the center, the subject of his movie, and the films explored motivation and consequences: the whys of the situation. Keaton was never as interested in the whys: he was more interested in the hows. Whereas Chaplin sought meaning, Keaton sought only function, his characters being there mainly to propel the mechanism of the comedy and the gags.

One might finally contrast their working techniques and characters. Chaplin was an obsessive perfectionist who would rehearse on film (an expensive practice) and do countless takes until he was satisfied the scene was right – by repute, one such scene in *A Woman of Paris* was shot 200 times. By contrast, Keaton would prefer to prepare in meticulous detail in advance and then do it in one take. 'For a real effect and to con-

vince people it's on the level, *do* it on the level,' he would say. 'No faking. Move the camera back and take it all in one shot.' There was sometimes a deeper philosophy to this. Sometimes a shot was so risky and dangerous – like the swing across the waterfall in *Our Hospitality* (1923) or the train falling through the bridge in *The General* (1926), or the house-front falling over his head in *Steamboat Bill Jr* (1928) – that a second take would probably either have been impossible or fatal.

Whereas Chaplin on a film set was serious, intellectual, clearly the leader, Keaton was apparently more of a team man, jovial, friendly, and gregarious. In miniature this expresses an important dimension of their personalities. As Chaplin's fame and artistic stature grew from such lowly origins, so did his sense of self-importance; he loved to be photographed and to exchange ideas with the most eminent men of the day: G B Shaw, H G Wells, Nehru, Picasso, Winston Churchill. By contrast, Keaton was a completely unpretentious man and genuinely bewildered by the attention given to him by the intellectual avant-garde. The great Spanish play-

BELOW: Hollywood at Hearst Castle. Buster is crouching, third from right; above him, to his right, is Greta Garbo. On the right, standing, Norma Shearer; below her sitting, Irving Thalberg. Lying on the ground is John Gilbert. Hal Roach is bottom left.

ABOVE: The family vaudeville act, when Buster was twelve. From left to right: Joe, Myra, Buster and Harry Keaton.

mystery in Keaton's screen persona, there came certain points in his life at which reality and disappointments impinged painfully, and the strain becomes evident in a more lined, flabbier face. Five years into talkies and with a monstrous movie like *What, No Beer?* (1933), Keaton at the age of 38 looked, according to the critic Gerald Mast 'less able, less physically alert than Chaplin looked in *Limelight* at 63.'

He was born Joseph Francis Keaton in 1895, and his childhood has two points of similarity with Chaplin's: they both were thrust on to the stage at an early age; and they both had alcoholic fathers. But whereas Chaplin's early years were mostly tragic and traumatic, Keaton's seem to have been very happy. Moreover, as a child, he led something of a charmed life. At the age of six months, he fell down a flight of stairs but emerged unscathed. 'That was some buster your baby took,' said his godfather, the escape-artist Harry Houdini, and the nickname stuck. This was as nothing compared with one memorable day at the age of three, when Buster was first hit by a brick on the head; then caught his finger in the wringer of a washing machine; and was finally lifted out of his bed by a tornado that flattened the entire town of Piqua but which reputedly deposited Buster, unharmed, four blocks away.

Keaton's mother and father were vaudevillians who were used to such bizarre events. The family were nearly trapped in three separate hotel fires, to the extent, said their father, that they habitually began to leave every hotel where they stayed by the fire escape rather than by the proper exit. 'Before I was much bigger than a gumdrop,' said Buster, 'I was being featured in our act. Even in my early days our turn established a reputation for being the roughest in vaudeville. Father began by carrying me out on the stage and dropping me on the floor. Next he started wiping up the floor with me. When I gave no sign of minding this he began throwing me through the scenery, out into the wings, and dropping me down on the bass drum in the orchestra pit. I didn't cry because I wasn't hurt . . . little kids when they fall haven't very far to go.' On one famous occasion, Keaton Sr even threw Buster into the audience to silence some hecklers who were sitting on the front row. Ribs were

wright, Federico Garcia Lorca, expressed his admiration in a short farce he wrote entitled 'Buster Keaton Takes a Walk,' while one of Buster Keaton's last film appearances, in the short *Film* (1965), was written for him by the author of *Waiting for Godot*, Samuel Beckett. Chaplin, or even Groucho Marx, might have professed to know Beckett's work or made an effort to master it, but Buster honestly confessed to never having read it and to not really liking or understanding the film. 'What I think it means,' he offered, 'is that a man can keep away from everybody, but he can't get away from himself.'

It is a comment with some relevance to Keaton's career and personality perhaps. For all the sense of detachment and

FAR RIGHT: Keaton, with cat, in *The Electric House*.

LEFT: On the right track: Buster Keaton in *The General*.

BELOW: Keaton acrobatics in *The Love Nest* (1923).

broken, but fortunately not Buster's.

One can certainly see here the origins of Buster's screen acrobatics, the ability to take a fall without fear or flinching. Apart from a single stunt in *College* (1927), where the hero has to pole-vault through a window and Buster substituted the Olympic champion Lee Barnes for the jump because 'you've got to get somebody who knows what they're doing,' Buster did all his most hair-raising stunts himself. Although he calculated he must have broken every bone in his body at some stage or another, he thought his only serious injury was breaking his leg on the electric staircase in *The Electric House* (1922) – until, that is, it was discovered that he must have broken his neck during a stunt in *Sherlock Jr* (1924) and not known of the injury until years after. Whereas an audience rooted for Harold Lloyd because his stunts always looked incredibly difficult and dangerous, Keaton had the knack of making the physically impossible look quite natural. This might actually have been something of a drawback to his popularity. Audiences of the time were more impressed by Harold

Lloyd's stunts than Keaton's because they could more easily empathize and identify with the difficulty the hero was experiencing. Keaton made the difficult look so easy that one's instinctive response was admiration more than sympathetic laughter.

Something else emerged from Buster's childhood performance as either the human projectile or the Human Mop. 'One of the first things I noticed,' he said, 'was that whenever I smiled or let the audience suspect how much I was enjoying myself, they didn't seem to laugh as much as usual. . . . It was on purpose that I started looking miserable, humiliated, hounded and haunted, bedeviled, bewildered and at my wit's end.' From here derives that deadpan expression, the serious solemnity with which the mature Buster Keaton would confront the camera and which seemed to say so much. 'His face went with the silence,' said Keaton's biographer, Rudi Blesh. 'Its motionlessness and the film's soundlessness compounded each other. Its immobility compelled attention, its expression compelled sympathy.' When asked once why he never smiled on camera, Keaton replied simply: 'I have other ways of showing I'm happy.'

Because his father's drinking made their vaudeville act progressively more hazardous, Buster eventually took over as the star of the show but was also looking to try another branch of showbusiness. His break came when he met Roscoe (Fatty) Arbuckle, who was making films for a motion picture company managed by Joe Schenck (who later became Buster's brother-in-law when Buster married the actress Natalie Talmadge and Schenck her sister, Norma Talmadge). 'Arbuckle asked me if I had ever been in a motion picture,' recalled Buster, 'and I said, "no, I hadn't even been in a studio." And he said, "well, come on down to the studio Monday and do a scene with me or two and see how you like it".' Buster took to film work immediately, made his first appearance with Arbuckle in *The Butcher Boy* (1917), and was straight away interested, as he said, 'in the mechanics of it. I wanted to know how that picture got put together through the cutting-room, and the mechanics of the camera, which fascinated me the most.' He made a number of comedy shorts with Arbuckle, until the latter decided to go to

Paramount in 1919 and Schenck set up a new company to produce Keaton shorts. Keaton was always to acknowledge his indebtedness to Arbuckle. Like Chaplin who, despite his reputation of meanness, kept loyal collaborators and employees (like Edna Purviance) on his payroll until the end of their lives, Keaton stayed loyal to people who had helped him. When Arbuckle became involved in Hollywood's most notorious sex scandal in 1923, being accused of rape and homicide, Keaton stood by him; and when Arbuckle, though completely exonerated of all charges, was abused by the public and shunned by the industry, Keaton continued to support him financially and find him work.

Talking about the simplicity of his dra-

ABOVE: Sybil Seeley and Buster Keaton in *One Week*, his first two-reeler and described by one trade paper as 'the comedy sensation of the year.'

LEFT: Salute and kiss: Keaton and Marion Mack in *The General*.

matic design, Keaton would say about his films that, 'there were usually but three principals – the villain, myself, and the girl, and she was never important . . . The leading lady had to be fairly good-looking and it helped some if she had a little acting ability. As far as I was concerned, I didn't insist that she have a sense of humor.' The short films had a simple central premise (Buster builds a boat in his basement in *The Boat*, Buster is chased by the entire police force in *Cops*) which is then comically embellished and developed. The feature-length films had, as far as possible, a straight narrative line, which reached its perfect form in *The General* (Buster loves girl and engine, both of whom are kidnapped during the Civil War; Buster pursues them along the track deep into enemy lines, rescues them, then puts the engine – and plot – into reverse to return home). The films were generally structured around a challenge (Buster is

ABOVE: In *Sherlock Jr* Keaton plays a cinema projectionist who dreams himself into the film he is projecting.

LEFT: Keaton encircled by cops in *Cops*.

rebuffed in love, or work, and has to respond) and then a chase, in which Buster redeems himself. 'Must every film end in a chase?' moaned Chaplin during his period with Mack Sennett at Keystone. But Keaton liked ending his films on a chase and did it superbly in films like *Cops* or *Seven Chances*. 'It works so well,' he would say, 'because it speeds up the tempo, generally involves the whole cast, and puts the whole outcome of the story on the block.'

When asked about the conception of character, he would say that 'you lay out your character according to the situations you're going to get into.' Unlike Chaplin's Tramp who, in Keaton's words, 'starts and stays a bum at all times,' Keaton would vary the character's personality and social status to extract the maximum humor from the situation. In *The Navigator*, for example, it is important that the hero is not only foolish but rich. 'Rollo Treadway,' says a title about him, 'heir to the Treadway fortune –

ABOVE: Keaton in *The High Sign* (1921).

RIGHT: Keaton in *The High Sign*, a film he completed before *One Week* but whose release he delayed because he thought *One Week* was much better.

TOP LEFT: Keaton in *Seven Chances*.

LEFT: Waiting for the bride: Keaton in *Seven Chances*.

a living proof that every family tree must have its sap.' If he had been a laborer, or poor, argued Keaton, then to be adrift on an ocean liner might not be so bad. It only becomes potentially funny if he is wealthy and has never had to lift a finger to do anything, and then suddenly finds himself adrift on a dead ship.

The themes and situations that Keaton returned to were fairly conventional: family rivalry; the conflict between father and son, and old and new; the little man struggling against the forces of nature. Keaton's screen character was an essentially modest man. Although no one confronted the camera more openly than Keaton, so that we seem always to be looking into his big eyes and pale face more than his profile, he never seemed to be playing for sympathy. This has always been one of his strongest points as a performer for those critics who deplore Chaplin's sentiment, but it might also be the reason why he was less popular with audiences at the time than either Chaplin or Harold Lloyd. 'An altogether extraordinary emotional effect came from the dreamlike, obsessive, hallucinatory, repe-

tition of that strange frozen face,' said the film director Albert Lewin, who was to attempt to raise Hollywood's artistic profile with such films as *The Moon and Sixpence* (1942), *The Picture of Dorian Gray* (1945) and *Pandora and the Flying Dutchman* (1951). 'It was almost nightmarish – a phantasmagoria of masks.' His third wife, Eleanor, with whom Buster had a lasting and happy marriage, said Buster was never very good at going out and selling himself, and this reticence and air of shy retirement is reflected in his screen character. He was no macho man and would solve his problems less by strength and force of character than by unobtrusive, intuitive, often ingenious logic. This was in turn translated into the films, which impressed less through character or situation than through the astonishing ingenuity of their gags.

Much of his comic and visual inventiveness is already present in his short films. His first as a director, *One Week* (1921), created quite a stir through its ingenious situation (a husband builds his new home from plans a jealous rival has deliberately mixed up, so that, for example, the front door ends up on the second floor), and

RIGHT: Dinner for two on an ocean liner: Kathryn McGuire and Buster Keaton in *The Navigator*.

LEFT: Boiling his egg in the ship's giant pan: from *The Navigator*.

RIGHT: Taking a spill in *The Navigator*.

through some brilliant visual comedy. At the end of the film they find their house is on a railway track, sigh with relief when an oncoming train veers on to an alternative track, only to find that their house is then flattened by a train coming from the other direction. *The Playhouse* (1921) took slapstick to the point of surrealism as Keaton plays all the parts – the film was intended as a satire on the silent director, Thomas Ince, who seemed to dominate the credits of his films – and at one stage, in an astonishing trick shot involving multiple exposures, plays nine musicians simultaneously. In *Cops*, Keaton got accidentally caught up in an anarchist's plot and was chased by the entire police force. The exhilaration of the chase is matched only by the Kafkaesque dimensions of the concept, as modern man seems endlessly pursued by the law, or by fate. In life, as in his films, Keaton was a fatalist. While relishing the athleticism and aplomb with which this poker-faced personality with the flat hat (that seemed as deadpan as himself) dodged his Nemesis, audiences seemed to feel a melancholy beneath the mirth and a

humor almost too clever to be cathartically comic.

Between 1923 and 1928 Keaton made 12 features of a sustained brilliance well nigh unmatched in film comedy. Some of the physical and visual routines were nothing short of astounding. In *The Three Ages* (1923), for example, Keaton's parody of D W Griffith's *Intolerance*, there is one remarkable routine where, in one single unbroken movement, Keaton, in escaping from a police station, climbs on to a roof, leaps across to a ledge, falls three storeys and grabs a drainpipe which breaks away and propels him through a window and into a fire station where he slides down the pole onto an engine which is setting out to put out a fire – at the police station from which he has just escaped. In *Our Hospitality* (1923), he swings himself astonishingly across a waterfall to catch his girl before she plunges to the torrents below. During the cyclone scene of *Steamboat Bill Jr*, the side of a house blows down over Buster who is saved because he is standing exactly at the spot where the open window falls – a stunt which, if Keaton had moved a matter of inches to either side, would undoubtedly have killed him. In *Sherlock Jr* (1924), there is an extraordinary moment where Buster as a film projectionist falls asleep and dreams himself into the picture he is projecting. In a double exposure shot his spirit seems to rise from his body and walk on to the cinema screen where he is suddenly threatened by the film's rapid montage, leaps of time and change of scene as, in consecutive shots, he is surrounded by desert, the ocean, a snowdrift, and a den of lions. It is not surprising that Albert Lewin was to describe Keaton as 'a surrealist even before surrealism.'

The Navigator (1924) was Keaton's most popular feature and it does have some superb visual conceits, like the scene in which the hero attempts to cook an intimate breakfast in a huge kitchen that is more used to catering for a thousand people than for a couple: the saucepan for the boiled egg is enormous. In *Seven Chances*, as a bachelor who stands to inherit a fortune if he can find a wife within 24 hours, he is chased by an army of voracious viragos intent on his money, probably the best chase sequence of his career. His best feature was probably *The General* (1926)

ABOVE: How to be a
detective: *Sherlock Jr.*

FAR LEFT: Buster Keaton
and Kathleen Myers in
Go West.

RIGHT: Keaton to the
rescue in *Steamboat
Bill Jr.*

ABOVE: Keaton on
parade in
The General.

RIGHT: The American
Civil War is the
background for Keaton's
greatest comedy, *The
General*.

because of its narrative logic, its visual beauty, and its apotheosis of the Keaton persona, who will scrutinize a problem and then solve it in the most imaginative way, whether it be the removal of an obstacle on the railway track or the maneuvering out of a room of two youngsters who are interrupting his courting. 'A page from history' was Keaton's description of the film and, although neither popular with the public nor acclaimed by the press, *The General* is now widely regarded as not only the greatest of silent film comedies, but the best film ever made about the American Civil War.

'The biggest mistake I made in my career,' Keaton was to say, 'was leaving my own studio and going to MGM. Chaplin warned me, so did Lloyd – but Joe Schenck talked me into it. And it wasn't that they didn't try, but those types of pictures and those little independent companies working – you could do better.' The first two

MGM films, *The Cameraman* (1928) and *Spite Marriage* (1929) had intermittent flashes of authentic Keaton magic, but the following films were very disappointing, and today almost forgotten, and Keaton was reduced to playing the straight man to Jimmy Durante in movies such as *Speak Easily* (1932) and *What, No Beer?* (1933). His problems were exacerbated by the painful break-up of his marriage to Natalie Talmadge, which, together with his career in the doldrums, tipped him over into alcoholism. There was also the problem of the talkies.

Keaton always claimed that the coming of sound to the cinema should have caused no difficulty for his screen style, for why could he not stay silent and let the sound go on around him? Still, it is hard to imagine those bone-crushing stunts of his having quite the same magic with added sound effects. Moreover there was some-

thing about Keaton's whole demeanor that seemed more properly to lend itself to the era of silents than of sound. 'He was by his whole style and nature,' said James Agee, 'so much the most deeply "silent" of the silent comedians that even a smile was as deafeningly out of key as a yell.'

While at MGM in the 1930s he had a spell as a gagman for the Marx Brothers on films such as *A Day at the Races, At the Circus*, and *Go West*. Groucho credited Keaton with being able to think up some good bits of business for Harpo, because he didn't talk or need lines, but otherwise looked on Buster as an anachronism. 'Is this supposed to be funny?' Groucho would say to Buster, as finicky about his scripts as W C Fields, who would often complain about scripts submitted to him that they were more suitable for Shirley Temple. 'I'm only doing what Mr Mayer asked me to do,' Buster would reply, with characteristic

ABOVE: Keaton in *Spite Marriage* (1929), his last major film as star.

RIGHT: Arrested motion: Keaton in *The Cameraman* (1928).

equanimity. 'You guys don't need any help.'

His declining career received something of a fillip from the praise lavished on him by James Agee in his classic 1948 article 'Comedy's Great Era' for *Life* magazine; from a cameo appearance in Billy Wilder's classic Hollywood exposé, *Sunset Boulevard* (1950); and from his wonderful comedy routine in the final part of Chaplin's *Limelight*. By the time of his death in 1966, he would have been heartened by the rediscovery of his work, even if it had come, as he put it, 'thirty years too late.' His last major public appearance was at the Venice Film Festival of 1965 where he was visibly moved by the prolonged standing ovation he received. 'This is the first time I've ever been invited to a film festival,' he said, 'but I hope it won't be the last.' It was.

Keaton's prowess as a comedian was undoubtedly nourished by his vaudeville up-

bringing with his father (sample joke: 'What makes you so small?' 'I was raised on condensed milk.') But, unlike Chaplin, Keaton's future development as a performer and a director owed very little to vaudeville and everything to a quintessentially cinematic skill in using the film frame for full effect. A modern director like Richard Lester has said how he can look at a Keaton film over and over and marvel at his camera-placement, his use of space within the frame, and his economy of style that would make every shot essential. For all Chaplin's dexterity as a director, his camera is ultimately there to record a performance. Keaton was interested in the camera as a marvelous instrument in its own right, which accounts for some of the startling visual effects of *The Playhouse* and *Sherlock Jr.* For some critics, although his themes might be contemporary, Chaplin's methods still reek of the conventions of Victorian melodrama where Keaton, although his themes are simple, unpretentious, and apolitical, has the mechanical mastery of a new medium for a new age. Keaton made motion pictures, whereas Chaplin made emotion pictures.

The complementary nature of their cinematic skills and personality has been nicely defined by the American critic,

Andrews Sarris. 'The difference between Keaton and Chaplin,' he said, 'is the difference between poise and poetry, between the aristocrat and the tramp, between adaptability and dislocation, between man as machine and man as angel, between the girl as a convention and the girl as an ideal, between life as farce and life as fantasy.' It does seem hauntingly appropriate that they should wind up sharing the same dressing-room in *Limelight*, the two giants of silent comedy, now ageing maestros preparing, to all intents and purposes, for their farewell performances. Both were now old men, happily married, having known the best of life and a bit of its worst, and having come through with dignity and serenity. At the end of his autobiography, Chaplin movingly counted his blessings and contemplated a belated contentment. Similarly with Buster Keaton. 'Because of the way I looked on the stage and screen,' he said, 'the public naturally assumed that I felt hopeless and unloved in my personal life. Nothing could be farther from the fact. As long back as I can remember, I have considered myself a fabulously lucky man.' Rather it is we who are the lucky ones: watching Keaton at his finest is both a privilege and a pleasure.

BOTTOM: Buster Keaton in *Sherlock Jr.*

CHAPTER THREE

Harold Lloyd
and Harry Langdon

It would be an exaggeration to say that Harold Lloyd and Harry Langdon are two of the forgotten men of early screen comedy, languishing under the shadow of the astounding genius of Chaplin and Keaton. It would be truer to say perhaps that they are somewhat underrated clowns whose ingenious routines can still surprise and dazzle modern audiences who might be discovering and experiencing their skills for the first time.

What is sometimes forgotten is that, in their heyday, Lloyd and Langdon were considered as great rivals to Chaplin and Keaton. Langdon had a golden period between 1924 and 1928 which, if sustained, might have made him an unqualified comic great. Harold Lloyd was always more popular with audiences during this period than Keaton; and also, because he made 11 features during the decade to Chaplin's three, even earned more than Chaplin himself. At the height of his popularity in 1926 Lloyd was earning $40,000 a week, whereas Chaplin – widely regarded as the best-loved and best-known personality in the world – was having to make do with a mere $30,000 a week.

What is more, Lloyd and Langdon seemed to offer a genuine alternative to Chaplin and Keaton. For some, if you wanted Chaplin's mastery of mime without his mawkishness, you could turn to Harry Langdon. If you preferred the daring athleticism of Keaton but with a little less mathematical detachment and a bit more emotional involvement, you could turn to Harold Lloyd. There was no real depth to Lloyd – he lacked the social commentary of Chaplin, or the occasional Kafkaesque gravity of Keaton – but, for many, that was all to the good. The humor was simple, direct, and exciting. 'If great comedy must involve something beyond laughter,' said the critic and screenwriter James Agee, 'Lloyd was not a great comedian. If plain laughter is any criterion – and it is a healthy counterbalance to the other – few people have equaled him and nobody has ever beaten him.'

Harold Lloyd was born on 20 April 1893.

ABOVE: Harold Lloyd.

He was the son of an unsuccessful photographer who, on moving to San Diego, had become a pool-hall proprietor. Lloyd had begun acting in small parts in touring companies and then in 1912 had made his screen debut with the Edison Company playing a Red Indian. An unsuccessful period with Mack Sennett's Keystone Company followed (Sennett was later to describe Lloyd as 'the one that got away'). His first major break came when he was hired by a friend and former Keystone extra, Hal Roach, who had gone into production. For Roach, Lloyd had some success with a character called Willie Work and then even more success with one

RIGHT: Harry Langdon, hiding, in *The Chaser* (1928).

called Lonesome Luke. Yet Lloyd had a niggling dissatisfaction with the role: it felt less like an individual character of his own devising than a superior Chaplin imitation. The point was underlined for him, he said, when he heard two boys debating whether to go to see the latest Lonesome Luke movie and, when one asked who the character was, the other replied: 'you know – the one who imitates Charlie Chaplin.' The influence of Chaplin on all film comedians at this time was immense, and enormously hard to escape.

Lloyd and Roach hit upon an alternative: the persona of an average man, mild-mannered, over-earnest perhaps, but a go-getter determined to succeed. Lloyd had recently been struck by a movie he had seen about a reticent bespectacled parson who had nevertheless taken on and ulti-mately defeated some die-hard ruffians. The most significant detail Lloyd took from this was not perhaps the man's manner so

LEFT: Going for a touchdown: Harold Lloyd in *The Freshman*.

BELOW: Harold Lloyd and bride (Jobyna Ralston) in *Girl Shy* (1924).

much as the spectacles, for Lloyd's most distinctive visual feature was to be his pair of large, horn-rimmed glasses. They were to become so inseparable a part of his persona that an audience would never question it when they popped up in the most unlikely of contexts. He sleeps with them on in *Kid Brother* (1927); wears them while fighting in *Grandma's Boy* (1921); and even plays football in glasses in *The Freshman* (1925), despite the fact that half his team has been flattened by the rough tactics of the other side. The screen was not to display a more charismatic and evocative pair of spectacles until the appearance of Woody Allen.

Explaining his appeal, Lloyd suggested that 'I represented a certain group. In my case it was young people working at a vocation and always struggling against a bigger guy.' Lloyd certainly had his own share of struggles. In 1920, when posing for a publicity shot for *Haunted Spooks*, a comedy bomb exploded and Lloyd lost his right thumb and forefinger. His right hand remained semi-paralysed and for a time it was feared he might lose his sight. Remarkably, after being hospitalized for nine months, he made an almost complete recovery. After being fitted with a surgical glove, he continued to do most of his stunts himself. There is something typical of the

ABOVE: John Aasen and Harold Lloyd in a potentially explosive situation in *Why Worry?* (1923).

screen Harold Lloyd about all this: perservering and indeed succeeding in spite of fearsome odds.

This determination was similarly echoed in his business enterprise within the film industry. In 1923 he began producing his own films and made a fortune from their release and re-release. (One of the reasons why they were subsequently less well-known than the Chaplins, the Keatons, and the Laurel and Hardys, was Lloyd's own zealous guarding of the film rights, and his reluctance to relinquish them to television or to release for use in extract form for film compilations of silent comedy.) He was a much shrewder businessman than, say, Buster Keaton or Harry Langdon. When he died of cancer at the age of 77 in 1971, he left $5 million to his heirs.

There is something about all this that was in the spirit of his films. In a comedy

form, he represented the success ethic of America, the wish-fulfilment of ordinary people. If he could make it, the films seemed to imply, who could not? Above all, Lloyd seemed a regular guy, the Jack Lemmon of his day, Mr Average America. Again it seemed symptomatic that whereas other silent comedians, like Chaplin, Keaton, Langdon and, most publicly and destructively of all, Fatty Arbuckle, were to have highly publicized difficulties with the opposite sex, the regular Mr Lloyd should marry his regular leading-lady, Mildred Davis, in 1923 and stay happily married to her for 46 years until her death in 1969.

'Lucky Lloyd,' one might say. Yet luck had little to do with Lloyd's success. He worked hard for it and, when it came, he worked hard to keep it. He closely supervised all his films and surrounded himself not only with gagmen but with writers whom he trusted and who understood the

persona Lloyd wanted to create and sustain. (Harry Langdon's failure to do that was arguably the major cause of his downfall.)

One example of Lloyd's filmic shrewdness was his use of the preview, testing his film in front of an audience before finally sending it out on release. (The producer Irving Thalberg was to credit Lloyd with introducing the film preview: whether it was indeed Harold Lloyd's innovation or not, he certainly used it extensively, and in due course it was to become an essential part

earlier been climbing inside his sweater. It is a brilliant visual joke but, after the preview, Lloyd significantly shortened it when he realized that the audience felt sorry for the character, which was something Lloyd did not want. He was out to avoid the pathos of Chaplin (and the accusations of Chaplin-imitation) at all costs. These are not sad comedies and to let an audience feel sorry for the hero, Lloyd felt, was not in character.

Conversely, the scene in the same film

of Hollywood studio procedure.) For example, when Lloyd discovered at a preview of his three reeler, *I Do* (1921), that audiences were bored, he threw out the opening reel and released it as a two reeler. In *The Freshman* there is a scene where the Lloyd character, Harold Lamb, offers to buy ice cream for all, and his entourage of immediate cronies swells and swells until he is being followed by seemingly the entire campus, including two kittens that had

where Harold Lamb's suit disintegrates at a dance, was extended after a preview to include the character's final indignity when his trousers fall down. Lloyd had wanted to avoid this low comedy cliché if at all possible, but he capitulated when previews told him that the scene got a much bigger laugh when it was included.

Lloyd was always alert to audience response. Given the stunts he involved himself with, it is surprising to learn that he

ABOVE: Harold Lloyd appearing in an early short film. Hal Roach is directing: Snub Pollard (with mustache and boater) is in the action. Bebe Daniels is the girl.

hated heights. His reasoning was that, if he were scared while doing this, the chances were that audiences would be as scared as himself. They would therefore identify all the more strongly with the hero and share his fear: his suspension, as it were, would add to the suspense.

Lloyd's most famous set piece is his scaling the wall of a skyscraper in *Safety Last* (1923), and it is worth discussing in some detail because it throws a great deal of light on Lloyd's methods, persona, and appeal. To begin with, it is a situation that Lloyd ensures is true to his screen character: that is to say he does not climb it because he wants to but to help someone else; a friend has been due to climb it but is being harried by the police. Lloyd will commonly act more out of friendship than of foolishness. The sequence is typical too of Lloyd's meticulous comic structure: he will get caught in a tennis net, be hit by popcorn and pigeons, be harassed by mice, dogs, and even an anemometer and, finally and most famously, find himself hanging off the clock face.

As he clutches the clock, the hands go backwards, then the whole face springs outwards: is our hero's time up? The scene is close to nightmare and it is not surprising to have seen it imitated in dramatic contexts, such as the most recent screen version of *The 39 Steps* (1978), where the hero, Richard Hannay (Robert Powell), has to cling to the hands of Big Ben and prevent their movement to twelve, by which they will detonate a bomb. One senses it was also an inspiration for the baroque clock-tower ending of Orson Welles's *The Stranger* (1946), in which Welles's Nazi villain is impaled by his beloved clock figures. Harold Lloyd as an inspiration for Orson Welles? It may seem far-fetched but Welles adored Lloyd's films, particularly *Safety Last*, which he thought 'one of the greatest, simplest films ever made.'

Another dimension of the sequence is its metaphorical implications. Might one take the whole situation as a metaphor for Lloyd's upward mobility, in the face of all the odds? One might make a mental comparison here with Jack Lemmon's hero in *The Apartment* (1960), a very Lloyd-like figure, an essentially small-town boy out to conquer the big city and doing so through working his way up a very tall building.

LEFT: Time on his hands: the famous moment when the clock face springs outwards in *Safety Last*.

terestingly similar to that of Alfred Hitchcock, who claimed that if you had four strong set-pieces in your movie, you had a good movie, and the trick was to build a solid enough structure around these sequences. Again Hitchcock might seem an incongruous comparison with Harold Lloyd. But Lloyd's most famous comedies were comedies of sensation, like *Never Weaken* (1921) or *Safety Last* (1923), thrill comedies with a high quotient of suspense. Lloyd always pointed out that comparatively few of his nearly three hundred films were like that, but the point is that the most memorable of them were. Even if he did not fully recognize it, suspense was to Lloyd what sentiment was to Chaplin: the engine of his humor.

Yet what about Lloyd's screen character himself? Was he funny, or did the humor reside essentially in what happened to him? Certainly in comparison with Chaplin, or Keaton, or Langdon, or the upcoming Laurel and Hardy, the Lloyd hero was basically an uncomplicated fellow. He was clean cut, having none of the lasciviousness of the tramp, the melancholy of Keaton, the sense of arrested development of Langdon. He was generally nervous and endearingly shy so that, for example, when he is unexpectedly called upon to make a speech in *The Freshman*, the audience goes out of focus.

Yet in the midst of this reticence, he was always ambitious. He was decent but determined. He was speedy, a man on the move, somebody who would make the final touchdown even if every player on the opposite side was sitting on top of him. In this he seemed to epitomize the optimism, energy, and exuberance of a burgeoning America. The critic Lewis Jacobs has pointed out how even the titles of many of his films seem to be moral exhortations: *Never Weaken, Now or Never, Welcome Danger, Get Out and Get Under*; and it might be here that we have the explanation for his phenomenal popularity of the time. He might not have been as great as Chaplin or Keaton, but he might have been closer to the mood and ideology of the time.

There were nevertheless some eminent critics who set their face firmly against Harold Lloyd. Gilbert Seldes described him as 'a man of no tenderness, no philosophy . . . there is no poetry in him, no overtone

ABOVE: Hanging on for dear life: *Safety Last*.

Lloyd was superb at devising images or situations that seemed quite natural metaphors for the nature of his heroes or the themes of his films. Think of the moment when he makes the winning touchdown in *The Freshman*, with practically the whole of the opposition on top of him and coming up with even the goal line stamped on him; a simple but eloquent image of victory against all the odds. It is a revealing contrast to Laurel and Hardy, whose goals seem, to ordinary eyes, perfectly feasible and achievable, but who rarely get past first base.

It is interesting that the sky-scraper sequence in *Safety Last* was conceived and shot first, and the rest of the film built around it. In explaining his method of comedy structure, Lloyd would talk of 'islands of four or five gags planned in advance – in between the islands you had to shift for yourself.' It is a view that is in-

ABOVE: Harold Lloyd in *Never Weaken* (1921), one of the first of his 'thrill' comedies, about a hero who attempts suicide when he thinks his girl has rejected him.

LEFT: *Never Weaken*: amazingly, Harold Lloyd had no head for heights.

LEFT: Harold Lloyd attempts to be an ardent lover in a screen test in *Movie Crazy* (1932).

RIGHT: Margaret Hamilton and Harold Lloyd in *Mad Wednesday*, directed by the redoubtable Preston Sturges and Lloyd's last starring role.

BELOW: Harold Lloyd being chicken in *Hot Water* (1924).

RIGHT BELOW: Jobyna Ralston and Harold Lloyd in *The Kid Brother*.

or image.' In a review of one of Lloyd's early talkies, *Movie Crazy* (1932), the critic and distinguished documentarian Pare Lorentz roundly declared that 'there is nothing funny about Harold Lloyd' and added that his manner 'suggests nothing so much as that of a live-wire insurance salesman.' He was a millionaire, Lorentz concluded, because he had learned long ago that 'rustics' will laugh if anyone 'falls on his rear, is kicked in the same spot, is hit over the head with a hard instrument, or makes a fool of himself over a girl.'

But there was surely more to Lloyd than this. Perhaps he did not have the individual inventiveness or imagination of Chaplin or Keaton. Nevertheless, he created a distinctive persona for himself. He was an innovator, using the preview more constructively than any previous director; abandoning two-reeler comedies after *Sailor Made Man* (1921) earlier than many

others and, in so doing, perhaps, influencing Chaplin's decision to expand the length of *The Kid* (1921). His antics on the sports field in *The Freshman* may well have had an influence on Buster Keaton's *College* (1927). Moreover he was quite popular in the sound era, adjusting to the new technology with some skill, and bowing out on a high note with an appearance in a film of that master film satirist (alas not at his best) Preston Sturges, *Mad Wednesday* (1948). He side-stepped controversy, unlike Chaplin, and kept creative and commercial control of his product, unlike Keaton, Langdon, and, later, Laurel and Hardy. Crucially, he knew his limitations and he knew his craft. If the persona finally seemed so right, the reason was that his progress mirrored in miniature the development of his own career: someone who made it the hard way but with dignity, and through a dogged, indomitable will to succeed.

LEFT: Harry Langdon in *The Strong Man*, directed by Frank Capra.

There is a moral here. To have talent is one thing: the trick is the ability, and opportunity, to make the most of it. There is no question about Lloyd's gifts: movies like *Safety Last*, *The Freshman*, and *Kid Brother* remain classics of screen comedy. But Lloyd nurtured his talent, protected it, lab-tested it, surrounded it with sympathetic and creative friends, and generally exploited it with a creative and commercial acumen. How different, then, from Harry Langdon, who had talent but who squandered it. He was 40 before he savored any real success, at which point his career suddenly soared. But in only four years, it was all to slip through his fingers. From the heights of triumph, Langdon was to descend into becoming what director Frank Capra called 'the most tragic figure I ever encountered in show-business.'

Born in Council Bluffs, Iowa, in 1884, Langdon worked, among other things, as a circus tumbler and strip-cartoonist before being spotted by Mack Sennett when doing vaudeville in Los Angeles. No doubt smarting from his failure to spot any comic potential whatever in Harold Lloyd, Sen-

nett felt that Langdon undoubtedly had something. The only problem for Sennett was that he could not put his finger on what it was. His enthusiasm was shared by Frank Capra who at that time was a young writer employed by Sennett and who, according to Sennett, 'wanted Langdon as soon as he set eyes on him.' 'Only God could help that man,' said one of Sennett's gag men in despair at finding any angle or line that could be exploited for Langdon. Capra immediately seized on that as the basis of Langdon's comic persona: that of a child-like elf whom only God could help. He was later to expand on the idea in an interview with James Agee. 'If there was a rule for writing Langdon material,' he said, 'it was this: his only ally was God. Langdon might be saved by a brick falling on a cop but it was *verboten* that he in any way motivated the brick's fall.'

Agee himself was to describe Langdon as seeming 'like an outsized baby who had begun to outgrow his clothes.' His moon-white face gazed out from under a hat whose brim was turned up all around. The hat never fitted snugly and neither did

RIGHT: Langdon in *Hallelujah, I'm A Bum* (1933).

anything else about him. The buttons of his coat were always in the wrong button-holes, and in general he had the appearance of a child who had for the first time tried to dress himself and failed. Complementing the child-like appearance was the comedy style, which was of a small-scale delicacy. His tiny gestures seemed to reflect the diminutive size of his brain, and Langdon's comic speciality was not the double- but the triple-take, because a thought or idea always took that little bit longer to get through to him.

Langdon shot into prominence with the success of three features. The first was *Tramp, Tramp, Tramp* (1926), directed by Harry Edwards from a script by Capra. When his father's livelihood is threatened, Langdon enters a marathon cross-country walking race, hoping to win the $25,000 prize money and also the love of the girl on the organizer's billboards (played by a young Joan Crawford). During his pilgrimage, he gets thrown into a chain gang and in an elaborate and beautifully timed sequence, inadvertently disarms the guard simply through the confusion he causes by choosing a tiny hammer to work with rather than the seldgehammer intended. Needless to say, Langdon does not use the gun that falls into his hand. He tosses it away and returns to his hammer, tapping it against a huge rock, as the film historian Kevin Brownlow deftly described it, 'like a child with an egg.' When it has no effect, he tries with a small pebble instead. It is a good example of the innocent, infant-like procedure of Langdon's character. Later in the film he has to contend with a cyclone. Originally Langdon was to point a gun at the cyclone in an endeavor to stop its progress, but Capra apparently suggested that

BELOW: A street cleaner in Chinatown: Langdon in *Feet of Mud* (1924).

this was too aggressive and not in character, for Langdon would never point a gun
at anything. In the final film, in a more
appropriately child-like (and much funnier) gesture, he throws little stones at the
impending storm. Miraculously, he succeeds in halting it in its tracks.

Langdon's child-like persona is developed still further in *The Strong Man* (1926),
which was Frank Capra's début as a director. We first see Langdon as a Belgian

soldier at the end of World War I, bombard-
ing his enemies not with bullets from a gun
but with biscuits from a catapult. After the
war, he searches for his penpal Mary
Brown, who turns out to be blind (perhaps
a forerunner of the blind flowergirl in
Chaplin's *City Lights*?) but before that, he
encounters one Broadway Lily (Gertrude
Astor), whose attempt to recover some
money by seducing him results in Langdon's having to fight for his honor. It is a

ABOVE: Langdon the
forlorn. The film
historian, William K
Everson called him the
'Carl Dreyer of the
clowns.'

LEFT: Caught on the high trapeze: Langdon in *Remember When*.

RIGHT: Surrounded by lovelies: Langdon in *The Head Guy*.

RIGHT: Langdon the lover: *Long Pants*.

scene that compares interestingly with a similar situation in the Laurel and Hardy film *Way Out West*, where the saloon girl Lola Marcel tries to regain some valuable deeds by vamping Stan Laurel (whose screen character was a kind of distant cousin of Langdon's). Laurel is merely reduced to a fit of giggles, but in the case of Langdon, you do have a sense that his innocence – hence his identity – is at stake.

The Strong Man, though, is most famous for its tremendous finale. Langdon is now an assistant to a Strong Man, who works in

a sin-ridden saloon, on the point of being stormed by outraged decent townsfolk. When the Strong Man falls drunk, Langdon has to take over and, finally, to quell the drunken audience's rage at his puny performance, fires a cannon that brings down the whole structure – much to the delight of the citizens outside, who see it as akin to the fall of the Walls of Jericho.

Langdon's following film, *Long Pants* (1927), was again directed by Capra. Again it has some charming moments, like the scene where Langdon cycles round his

LEFT: Amorous or murderous? Langdon seems to be taking the phrase 'shotgun wedding' somewhat literally in *Long Pants*.

loved one who is in a car, his pace slowing in direct proportion to the way his love is accelerating. But the tone of the film is harsher. Langdon is trying to kill off his girlfriend because he is enamored of a sexual siren. There are some humorous scenes of murderous incompetence, but the more astringent tone probably reflects the strained relationship that had developed between him and Capra, creative differences over the development of Langdon's screen character that had become more abrasive because of the egotistical nature of both men. Their relationship was to come to an acrimonious end after this film. Coincidentally, or significantly, depending on one's point of view, this was to be Langdon's last big success.

Whatever happened to baby Langdon? What went wrong? Perhaps there is a clue in an interview he gave to *Photoplay* in 1925. 'The oddest thing about the whole funny business,' he said, 'is that the public really wants to laugh but it's the hardest thing to make them do it. They don't want to cry, yet they will cry, at the slightest provocation. Maybe that's why so many comedians want to play tragedy – they want a sort of vacation.'

Langdon did not necessarily want to play tragedy but, according to Capra, he did want to inject more pathos into his films. He wanted indeed to out-Chaplin Chaplin – a big mistake, thought Capra. The difference was simple: Chaplin knew and understood everything about his own creation, whereas Langdon never really understood his own talent. So the two men argued, each claiming that one was stealing too much credit from the other, and went their separate ways. Capra went on to make imperishable classics such as *It Happened One Night* (1934), *Mr Deeds Goes to Town* (1936), *Mr Smith Goes to Washington* (1939), and *It's A Wonderful Life* (1946). By contrast, Langdon went on an arrow-straight path to oblivion. He directed himself in features such as *Three's a Crowd* (1927), *The Chaser* (1928) and *Heart Trouble* (1928), which have their admirers but are rarely revived and were not successful. His marriage broke up and in 1931 he filed for bankruptcy.

'He went Hollywood all of a sudden,' Capra said of Langdon at the height of his fame. 'He suddenly started to wear scarves and bright clothes. He bought a big house and discovered girls . . . People went crazy about this man and he just couldn't handle it. He couldn't handle the renown he was getting.' Whatever the reason, there is no doubt that Langdon's popularity declined sharply after the severing of his relationship with Capra. He was reduced to playing bit parts in the 1930s, for his slow-burn style and mastery of mime were alien to the kind of speed and verbal wise-cracking demanded in the new era of the talkies. He

BELOW: Langdon and Hardy in *Zenobia*. There were rumors that Langdon was to replace Stan Laurel as Ollie Hardy's partner, but they were unfounded.

LEFT: Langdon and
Charles Murray in
Flickering Youth.

did collaborate on the scripts of a number of Laurel and Hardy pictures, including *Blockheads* and *A Chump at Oxford*, and he did indeed deputize for Laurel, opposite Hardy, in one film, *Zenobia* (1939), which started a rumor that Hal Roach was planning to substitute Langdon as Hardy's new partner. But it was not to be.

It is tempting to think of Langdon as Laurel without Hardy. Alternatively he conjures up an image of Jerry Lewis in slow motion. For some critics there has always been an element of grotesqueness about Langdon, the overgrown baby (he reminded the critic Stuart Kaminsky of Bette Davis in *Whatever Happened to Baby Jane*). But within his particular range – less physically agile and expressive than Chaplin, Keaton or Lloyd – he had a rich talent and one of the most soulful faces of silent cinema.

Capra's last memory of Langdon was one of seeing a young director shouting 'faster, faster,' at the now ageing clown, when Capra was visiting a sound stage. 'You don't tell Langdon to go faster,' Capra muttered to himself, still paternalistically,

proprietorially guarding the character. 'You can only tell him to go slower.' Such an instruction could only come from a director, he thought, fundamentally out of tune with Langdon's style. It would be like asking Jack Benny to speed up his delivery.

'By the time I directed him in sound comedy,' said the experienced Eddie Sutherland, 'the poor man was a beaten, defeated fellow. Sound hurt Langdon too. He was not so funny articulate.' Unlike Lloyd, whose donnish appearance betokened a certain detachment and whose name 'Harold' had an undertone of formality (one never even thinks of him as 'Harry' Lloyd), Langdon always carried a certain vulnerability with him. Like a number of great comedians, he looked as if he could be hurt, fatally, inside. Neglected, forgotten, four times divorced, he died in 1944, unacknowledged, but destined to be revived in the esteem of a succeeding generation of film scholars and students. He is always being rediscovered, and re-evaluated. The last word is not yet in on Harry Langdon.

CHAPTER FOUR

Laurel and Hardy

An introductory title to the Laurel and Hardy comedy *The Hoosegow* (1929) runs as follows: 'Neither Mr Laurel nor Mr Hardy had any thoughts of doing wrong. As a matter of fact, they had no thoughts of any kind.'

Something of the essence of the screen's most successful partnership is in that statement. It seems to encapsulate both their absence of malice, which makes them sympathetic, and their absence of intelligence, which made them hilarious. It is also noteworthy that they are referred to as '*Mister* Laurel and *Mister* Hardy.' When Blake Edwards dedicated his big-budget slapstick comedy *The Great Race* (1965) to 'Mr Laurel and Mr Hardy,' the critic Kenneth Tynan upbraided him for being pompous and formal. But Edwards was being both historically accurate (this was always how Oliver Hardy would introduce them to others in their films) and paying homage to a singular quality in their personalities: their dignity. It was always an important part of their personalities. Hardy would

often *stand* on his dignity, which was particularly funny when it would then give way beneath his feet. But neither he, nor Laurel, ever lost it.

Laurel and Hardy were the movies' first successful comedy team and remain to this day its best, much imitated, never surpassed. The range of their appeal remains extraordinary. It embraces both child and adult, and tickles the fancy of the most lowbrow and highbrow of audiences (think of their acknowledged influence on such high-powered, intellectual avant-garde works like Samuel Beckett's *Waiting for Godot* and Eugene Ionesco's *Rhinoceros*). They were the perfect team because they were so complementary: fat/thin; pretentious/empty-headed; aspirations of 'superiority' and 'adulthood' (Hardy) against intimations of inferiority and childishness (Laurel). They looked funny together: as the critic and later screenwriter Frank Nugent pointed out, perhaps people have said too much about the anatomy of humor and not enough about the humor of anatomy. Laurel with his dumb smile, watery eyes, and clownish hair, Hardy with his roly-poly frame, ill-fitting clothes, and

LEFT: Oliver Hardy (left) and Stan Laurel (right) in *Sons of the Desert* (1934).

RIGHT: Returning from the convention to their long-suffering wives: Laurel and Hardy in *Sons of the Desert*, pretending they have actually been to Honolulu.

94

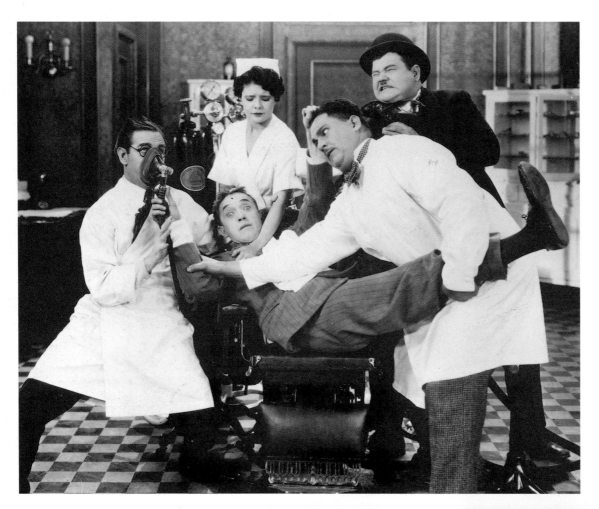

LEFT: Laurel creates havoc in the dentist's chair in *Leave 'em Laughing*.

BELOW: Laurel and Hardy buy a boat in *Towed in the Hole* and start to renovate it. As the still indicates, things do not run smoothly.

endlessly expressive face – their physical presence alone prompted a chuckle. Also, unusually in comedy teams, they were both equally funny, which, as the producer of their first successes, Hal Roach, said, was a tremendous bonus because it meant that every joke had that much more potential and resonance. For example, said Roach, if somebody falls into a ditch accidentally, there was usually the possibility of one laugh, but if Laurel or Hardy did it (and it was usually Hardy), there was the possibility of three laughs: the situation itself; Hardy's pained expression of affronted dignity; Laurel's expression of innocent mystification.

Together they seemed to embody the compromises of comradeship. They malfunctioned with each other, but could not function at all without each other. The Hollywood director of *The Blues Brothers*, John Landis, has put it this way: 'There is a loyalty that transcends all their trials. While it often seems that other comedy teams are together purely out of convenience, Stan and Ollie are an organic whole from the first frame of every picture. You

ABOVE: Another fine mess: Laurel and Hardy in *Their Purple Moment* (1928). (It should perhaps be noted that Hardy generally said: 'This is another *nice* mess you've gotten me into.')

LEFT: Spirit of Christmas: Laurel fights James Finlayson in *Big Business*.

never question their oneness.' At times they do seem two aspects of the same personality, and yet their coming together as a team was quite fortuitous: one might even call it fate.

There is a moment near the end of *Way Out West* (1937) when Oliver Hardy discovers that the damsel he and Stan have rescued from distress in Brushwood Gulch comes from the South. 'I'm from the South,' he crows, to which Stan insists that he is from the South also. When Hardy looks puzzled, Laurel says, by the way of explanation: 'London.' Not quite true, but it is a reminder of Stan Laurel's English origins as distinct from Oliver Hardy's background of the American South. As the background of both is significant in the ultimate definition of their screen characters, it is appropriate to say something more about it here.

Stan Laurel's real name was Arthur Stanley Jefferson, and he was born in Ulverston, Lancashire, on 16 June 1890. His father was a one-time actor, playwright, and well-known theatrical impressario, so it was no surprise that Stan was drawn to

show business. He made his stage début in Glasgow at the age of 16 under the name of Stan Jefferson, perhaps to distinguish himself from his father who was also called Arthur. However, early in his career, he superstitiously noted that his stage name 'Stan Jefferson' had 13 letters in it and he changed it to Laurel. 'Funny – I don't know why I picked Laurel,' he was to say later. 'Honestly can't remember. Just sounded good, I guess. However, my hunch was right. Things started to get better right away, and after I got known in pictures, I had my name legalized.'

Stan's route to the motion picture business was a relatively circuitous one. In England he had joined the famous Fred Karno Company in 1910 and had accompanied them on their American tour of that year, understudying their star comedian, a young man by the name of Charlie Chaplin. ('He was a very eccentric person then,' Laurel later recalled of Chaplin. 'He was very moody and often very shabby in appearance. Then suddenly he would astonish us all by getting dressed to kill. He read books incessantly . . . carried his violin wherever he could. Had the strings reversed so he could play left-handed, and he would practise for hours.') Chaplin and Laurel were never to become friends, but Laurel's admiration for him remained unbounded throughout his life: 'just the greatest,' he was to say of Chaplin. When Karno toured America again in 1912 with his *Night in an English Music Hall*, with Stan once again understudying Chaplin, Stan decided to settle in America.

He began appearing in films in 1917, including a now-lost two-reeler entitled *Lucky Dog*, in which he has a brief scene with a villainous outlaw played by none other than Oliver Hardy. But it was some time before their paths were to cross again on film. Indeed, it is sometimes forgotten that Stan Laurel had made 76 films before being teamed with Hardy, and was quite a successful film comedian in his own right, particularly those films in which he comically satirized some of the successes of the day. One of his best-remembered solo films, for example, is a parody of Rudolph Valentino's hit, *Blood and Sand*, called *Mud and Sand*, in which Stan Laurel played a character called 'Rhubarb Vaselino.' His

career was progressing pleasantly if uneventfully when, in 1926, he signed up with an old friend, Hal Roach, who had gone into production as a kind of rival to Mack Sennett, and who put Laurel into a film with another actor called Oliver Hardy. The film was *Putting Pants on Philip* (1926), in which Hardy played a respectable American and Laurel his womanizing Scottish nephew, Philip, who arrives in America wearing a kilt, much to everyone's amusement. As yet, the screen characters of Laurel and Hardy have not been formed: they do not use their own names in the film, and Stan's interest in girls is something he will drop from his later screen personality. But, as the critic Charles Barr has noted, in retrospect there was something fateful and allegorical about the film, as Oliver Hardy's dignified gentleman from the American South awaits the arrival of a 'relation' from Britain, who will in no time transform his life.

Oliver Norvell Hardy was born in Harlem, Georgia, on 18 January 1892. Although there was no precedent of any theatrical background in his family, unlike that of Stan Laurel, he did claim a curious English

LEFT: Lady in cement: Dorothy Coburn suffers the incompetence of Laurel and Hardy as building contractors in *The Finishing Touch* (1928).

ABOVE: Laurel and Hardy
join the Foreign Legion:
Beau Hunks.

connection by suggesting that he was descended from the Captain who had attended to Lord Nelson ('Kiss me, Hardy') when Nelson was dying during the Battle of Trafalgar. As a young man, Oliver thought of a career in law and even toyed with the idea of becoming a professional singer, for he had an excellent tenor voice (a skill that was later to be used in his films, of course). However, he became interested in films after he had opened the first movie theater in Milledgeville, Georgia, in 1910. When film work subsequently became available, he decided to try for it, and made numerous films, generally playing the heavy, prior to being signed up by Hal Roach in 1926. In his early films, he had been billed as Norvell Hardy or 'Babe' Hardy (which was a nickname from childhood), and later sometimes appeared under the billing of Oliver 'Babe' Hardy or Oliver N. Hardy. In his films for Roach, he

became Oliver Hardy, and that is how he stayed.

The screen personality of Oliver Hardy was, he said, developed partly out of himself and partly out of a cartoon character called 'Helpful Henry.' From his own personality, Oliver borrowed the Southern courtesy, and the sensitivity about his bulk. 'Helpful Henry,' whom Oliver had enjoyed reading in Georgia newspapers when a child was a character who, in Oliver's words, 'was always trying to be helpful, but he was always making a mess of things. He was very big and fussy and important but underneath it all he was a very nice guy.' That in essence was what Oliver Hardy was after in his own screen character: it was as simple as that.

It is well known that Stan was the comedy brains behind the team, and that Ollie, after doing his part, was content then to retire to the golf course (and also con-

LEFT: Street musicians of dubious delight: Laurel and Hardy in *You're Darn Tootin'*.

ABOVE: Repairing their boat: *Towed in the Hole*.

seriously, and because he never sees – and, still less, signals – the joke, the humor becomes all the funnier. It is something that a star film comedian of the 1930s Eddie Cantor commented on about Laurel and Hardy. 'It is their seriousness that strikes me most forcibly,' he said. 'They play everything as if it might be *Macbeth* or *Hamlet*.' This is particularly true of Hardy whose air of gravity and self-importance seems to cry out for puncturing. When the biographer John McCabe watched the films with Stan Laurel (and Laurel, ever the scientist of comedy, remembered literally every detail of the films), he was intrigued to find that Stan would watch Hardy more than himself. 'The guy fascinates me,' he said, by way of explanation. 'He really is a funny, funny fellow, isn't he?'

It was during their 27 silent shorts together, made between 1926 and 1929, that their screen personalities and partnership began to settle into the shape that we recognize with such affection today. It was particularly marked by small, almost Dickensian, characteristics that became indelible parts of their characters. In Oliver Hardy's case, for example, one came to look for, and love, that nervous little twiddle of the tie, which would sometimes

tent, according to some accounts, to receive half the salary of Laurel per picture). Curiously, Oliver Hardy never thought he was funny at all, and saw himself merely as a cog in the machine, the straight man, the fall guy to Stan Laurel's comic clown. 'He never truly considered himself a comedian at all,' said his wife, 'and he was genuinely surprised that people thought of him as such.' It might be that is precisely the secret of his success. Because he takes himself so signify self-satisfaction but more often embarrassment, or those neat little hand movements, whether driving a car or signing a hotel register with an elaborate flourish, that betokened his pretence, or aspirations, of gentility. Most particularly there were his looks at the camera – of resignation, disbelief, outrage, exasperation – that seemed to invite us to become accomplices in his frustration with his friend, to share his stoical endurance of life's misfortunes. That kind of inner, slow-burning, intimate stoicism is a rare quality in screen acting. For tiny facial nuance – the ability to convey an infinity of emotion with the minimum of means, through a single close-up – Hardy was almost unmatched in the heyday of Hollywood, with perhaps the single exception of Spencer Tracy. Indeed, one can see something of Hardy's influence in Spencer Tracy's acting in the famous final scene of *Woman of the Year* (1941), as he sits with quiet endurance as his wife (Katharine Hepburn), aiming to prepare his breakfast, succeeds only in wrecking the kitchen. A fanciful connection? Perhaps not, when one recalls that the director of the film, the great George Stevens, had got his start in

movies through photographing such classic Laurel and Hardy shorts as *Putting Pants on Philip*, *The Battle of the Century* (1927) and *Big Business* (1929).

In the case of Stan Laurel, one began also to recognize bits of comic business that helped to define the character. There was, for instance, the empty-headed gesture of simultaneously scratching his head and pulling up his wild hair, which seemed an indicator of his dimwittedness. The inspiration for it had come after Stan, having played a convict in a two-reeler and having obligingly had his hair shaved to a crew-cut for the role, found his hair impossible to control when it started to grow back. Noticing that his attempts to control it only increased an observer's laughter, he kept things as they were: the upraised hair became a trademark. As John McCabe remarked, 'it gave him, in effect, a natural fright wig – a sure laugh getter . . . The raised hair in turn emphasized his lean features and triangular chin, thus making him the stuff of which brilliant caricatures are made.' Another trademark was the child-like 'cry' when upset. It was a bit of business that Stan himself never particu-

BELOW: Taking the high road: Jimmy Finlayson (left) and Laurel and Hardy in *Bonnie Scotland*.

larly liked, but it was loved by audiences. Moreover it did seem to define the character ever more precisely: basically that of a child, an innocent, who is bossed by a headmasterly, quasi-parental big-brother figure who, in fact, is hardly more capable or mature than he is. 'We were dignified but dumb,' said Stan, when defining the essence of their characters. 'I haven't a lick of commonsense and Ollie is just as dumb, but he thinks he's smarter.'

As well as demonstrating a steady development and perfection of the characters, the silent shorts also began to elaborate a classical structure that was to be the basis of most of their best films: a logical, step-by-step movement from a mistake to a catastrophe. A harmless scheme will end up encountering a whirlwind of social hostility. An initially perfect day will end up as a disastrous nightmare. The boys will begin with next to nothing and end with less than nothing.

There are numerous examples of that basic structure in these early silent shorts. In *Leave 'em Laughin'*, directed by Clyde Bruckman in 1928, they are given too much laughing gas at the dentist, a situation that

RIGHT: The custard pie fight to end all custard pie fights: *The Battle of the Century*. Mack Sennett was to call it 'custard's last stand.'

103

escalates into total mayhem among the city traffic. In *You're Darn Tootin'* directed by Edgar Kennedy in the same year, they are seemingly harmless street musicians who, by the end, are responsible for street chaos and for everyone losing his trousers.

The two most famous examples of this from this period are *The Battle of the Century* (1927) and *Big Business* (1929). In *The Battle of the Century* Stan plays a boxer and Ollie is his manager, but the early plot development is completely subsumed by an epic pie-throwing concluding sequence, which attempts to out-Sennett Sennett. Blake Edwards was to pay homage to that sequence in the afore-mentioned *The Great Race* – in wide-screen and color – and the writer Henry Miller was to remark that *The Battle of the Century* was 'the greatest comic film ever made – because it brought the pie-throwing to apotheosis.' No less remarkable was *Big Business*, in which Laurel and Hardy play Christmas-tree salesmen in July (they are often to be found in comically incongruous employment, as in *Below*

Zero, where they play street buskers singing 'In the Good Old Summertime' in sub-zero temperatures, or in *Swiss Miss*, where they play mousetrap salesmen in Switzerland). A simple argument with the feisty James Finlayson develops into a gigantic conflict that ends with the destruction of a house and a car. As the documentary film-maker Basil Wright has observed, its 'absurdity' does not disguise an underlying truth of how easy it is for a small conflict to swell into something more serious. Wright sees the film, convincingly enough, as a parable of escalating warfare.

As we have seen, the transition from the silent to the sound era of film caused a great deal of difficulty for some of the major screen comics of the 1920s, like Chaplin (who loathed the talkies), Keaton (whose stone-faced stoicism ill-fitted the new talkative era) and Lloyd (who had a high-pitched voice that irritated some critics). But sound caused no problems for Laurel and Hardy: the various creative problems in their later career were to come from other

BELOW: Hardy is brained by Swiss cheese in *Swiss Miss*. Laurel, on the other hand, has a brain *like* Swiss cheese – full of holes.

LEFT: Inefficient bodysnatchers in *Habeas Corpus*.

sources entirely. Indeed, one could say that sound actually enhanced their comedy. Both of them had good speaking voices, which ideally matched their screen personalities. Moreover Ollie had a splendid singing voice which he could unfurl on certain occasions, nowhere more memorably than in *Way Out West* when he picks up a cowboy's refrain and launches into a most melodious rendering of 'The Trail of the Lonesome Pine.'

They were similarly astute with dialogue. Both of them had exquisite timing but, quite properly, they saw that dialogue should be used in their films more as atmosphere and punctuation than as exposition or comedy: the emphasis of their humor was still visual. Nevertheless, there are still some exquisite little dialogue exchanges that are very revealing of character, particularly of Stan Laurel's child-like literalness, his difficulty with language making proverbs and idiomatic turns of phrase particularly hard for him to comprehend. 'Upset? Why, I'm housebroken!' he exclaims in *Babes in Toyland* (1934). When he and Ollie are up before a judge on a vagrancy charge in *Scram* (1932), the judge asks if they are pleading guilty or not guilty. 'Not guilty,' says Ollie. 'On what

ABOVE: A classic scene from *Swiss Miss* in which they attempt to transport a piano across a rickety bridge.

grounds?' asks the Judge. 'We weren't on the ground, we were sleeping on a park bench,' replies Stan, with the exasperating literal logic that is so much a part of him. The important thing here is that he is not trying to be funny: it is simply the way his mind works. His literalness in *Way Out West* will lead him into a situation where he has literally to eat Ollie's hat. In *Helpmates* (1931), when they are having an argument during the tidying of Ollie's flat, Stan says:

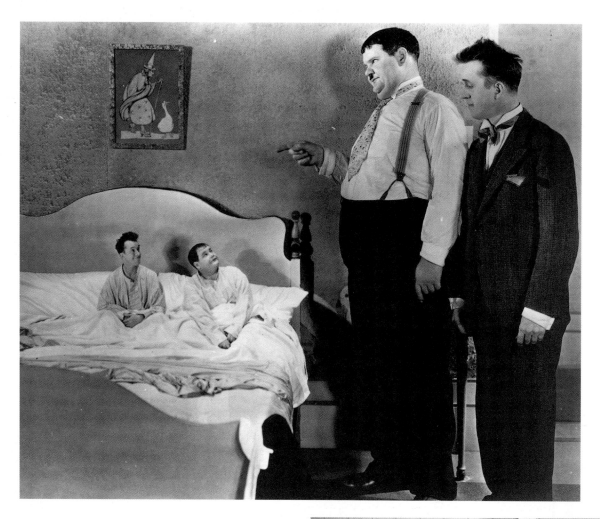

LEFT: Laurel and Hardy with their identical offspring in *Brats*.

BELOW: Bedtime for children: *Brats*.

'You know, if I had any sense, I'd leave.' 'Well, it's a good thing you haven't,' replies Ollie, to which Stan replies triumphantly: 'It certainly is!' It takes a while for him to notice that the argument has not been as successful as he first thought, and, minutes later, we see him still rehearsing the argument, trying to find the flaw in the logic, wondering where he went wrong. Suddenly in those watery eyes, that slight drawl, the slow thought processes, we have a ghostly premonition of a young Jimmy Stewart.

The Laurel and Hardy films of this period – the early 1930s – also used sound very creatively and comically. The use of off-screen sound was often as funny as the dialogue or even the visuals. In *Helpmates*, Stan Laurel has just finished washing a huge pile of dishes: in the next room, Oliver Hardy slips on a roller skate and goes flying through the open door; we *hear* the crash before we see the devastation. In *County Hospital* (1932), Stan drops the egg he has been painstakingly peeling, and we hear a very suggestive tinny sound to hint at where the egg has landed. It actually turns out to be Ollie's water jug rather than his bedpan, but the association of thought is continued when Ollie, meting out

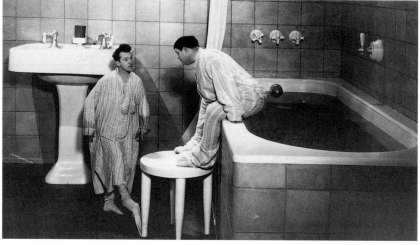

punishment, hits Stan with the pan.

The delights of these shorts are too numerous to give other than a sketchy impression. In *Habeas Corpus* (1928), Stan and Ollie are employed as bodysnatchers but become completely spooked by the graveyard they are robbing, particularly when Stan inadvertently puts his lamp down on the shell of a tortoise and, when it starts moving, thinks the graveyard is haunted. *Night Owls* (1930) has them trying to break into a house with singular ineptitude, and then trying to put James Finlayson's bodyguard off the scent by simulating cat noises. In *Brats* (1930), they play their own

ABOVE AND RIGHT: On the town: Ollie Hardy and Stan Laurel entertain two ladies in *Men o' War*. James Finlayson is the bartender.

RIGHT AND BELOW:
Delivery men in *The Music Box* for householder Billy Gilbert.

sons as well as themselves and, of course, behave more childishly as adults than they do as children, while in *Our Wife* (1931), when Ollie is getting married and Stan is the best man, a cross-eyed magistrate (Ben Turpin) manages to get the two married to each other. There is a hilarious scene in *Men o' War* (1929) when they play sailors on leave and Ollie finds he has not enough money to pay for drinks for himself, Stan, and the two girls they have picked up. Stan consistently misunderstands Ollie's desire that he should refuse his request for a drink, and when they finally hit upon the compromise of agreeing to share one, Stan

promptly drinks it all, explaining that he couldn't help it – his half of it was on the bottom.

One of the duo's most spectacular (and dangerous) visual jokes occurs at the end of *Busy Bodies* (1932). 'What a beautiful morning . . . why, even you look bright this morning,' Ollie has said to Stan, as they are on their way to a new job at a sawmill. The day, however, is destined to be a disaster (they burst a pipe, Ollie gets trapped in a window frame, they squabble with each other and workmates, being assailed by them with a variety of weapons, including sticky brushes and planks of wood). It seems nothing else can go wrong until they step into their car – which is slowly sawn in half by a mechanical saw.

Perhaps their best-remembered short, however, and their only Oscar winner, is *The Music Box* (1932), in which, as removal specialists for the Laurel and Hardy Transfer Company (their motto: 'Tall Oaks from Little Acorns Grow'), they attempt to move a piano up a massive flight of steps. This is, in fact, only half the film: later they will discover a much easier route, and there will be a superb scene when they tidy up with choreographic precision to the music from the music box, their best dance sequence

prior to their soft-shoe shuffle outside the saloon bar in *Way Out West*. But it is the first part one particularly remembers, because it is quintessential Laurel and Hardy: the absurd task, which they tackle with an earnestness that is surpassed only by the scale of their incompetence. The film historian William K Everson wittily described it as a 'light-hearted equivalent of the Odessa Steps sequence in Eisenstein's *Potemkin*.' The step-ladder seems almost to symbolize Stan and Ollie's path through life: the harder they try to get to the top with the burden, the more surely are they obstructed or pushed down again to the bottom – and they could have gone round anyway.

'We should have stayed in the short-film category,' Stan Laurel was to say. 'There is just so much comedy we can do along a certain line and then it gets to be unfunny. You've got to settle for a simple basic story in our case and then work out all the comedy that's there – and then let it alone.' For Stan, the biggest mistake they made in their career was to expand into feature-length films. Curiously, Ollie disagreed with him and according to his wife, Ollie's favorites among the films were those that had 'production,' that incorporated more

than straight comedy. 'He always felt that in feature films,' she said, 'the comedy should be incidental to the story and overall production – that the comedian or comedians shouldn't be forced to carry the whole load of the film.' But Stan felt that their style was not really suited to feature-length and that, as he said about their first full-length feature, *Pardon Us* (1931), they were constructing a 'three-storey building on a one-storey base.'

Hal Roach thought that part of the problem was that it did expose one of Stan's weaknesses as an inventor of comedy – that while he was brilliant on detail and

ABOVE: Teacher James Finlayson points an accusing finger at Laurel and Hardy in their first feature *Pardon Us*.

comic business, he was less good on narrative development. When one reviews the films, one is also struck by the fact that, in the feature films, Stan and Ollie are surrounded by supporting players who are often second-rate: the romantic leads, for example, are often distinctly unappealing. It was a problem that was to bedevil the Marx Brothers: in attempting to broaden their appeal, the studio succeeded mainly in diluting their comedy. So there is much dross in the Laurel and Hardy features, but there is much that is treasurable also.

The two best features are probably *Sons of the Desert*, also known as *Fraternally Yours* (1933), and *Way Out West* (1937). In the former, Laurel and Hardy are members of a Masonic fraternity called 'Sons of the Desert' (in real life Ollie was a Mason) and they wish to attend the annual convention without informing their wives. Needless to say, massive complications ensue. It is one of their most tightly plotted films and has quite large roles for their wives, fearsome matriarchs dedicated to whipping the boys

back into line. Ollie does some priceless looks at the camera, particularly at the activities of his brother-in-law (Charley Chase) at the convention, and some incredibly delicate finger gestures of drumming on the table or twiddling with his tie as he apprehensively awaits retribution from his wife who has seen through his deceit. Stan is particularly fine in the early part of the film when he colludes with Ollie in concocting an illness that will require a recuperative Honolulu cruise, providing an excuse to slip out to the convention. Stan takes Ollie's temperature with a barometer. 'What does it say?' Ollie asks. 'Wet and windy,' replies Stan, nonchalantly. They contrive to bring in a fake doctor to assist their scheme, but Stan's choice proves to be somewhat inapposite. 'Why did you get a veterinarian?' asks Ollie huffily, to which Stan replies: 'Well, I didn't think his religion would make any difference.' The comedy at the convention is finely sustained and a lavish musical number, 'Honolulu Baby,' even summons up an

TOP LEFT: Tripping the light fantastic in *Way Out West.*

BELOW: Champagne time: *Sons of the Desert.*

elaborate aerial shot that is pastiche Busby Berkeley.

Way Out West is perhaps less ingenious, imaginative and intricate as a narrative, but it has some delightful moments: for example, Stan attempting to thumb a lift from a stagecoach (when that fails, he shows a leg); a hilarious shot of Stan, Ollie and a mule haring down a flight of steps (Ollie is later to call Stan, even with this mule between them, as 'the dumbest thing I ever saw'). Ollie attempts to charm a lady on the stagecoach with such conversational gambits as 'a lot of weather we've been having lately,' and 'It's only four months to Christmas.' The plot has to do with their delivery of the deeds to a valuable gold mine to a young lady called Mary Roberts, and the attempt of James Finlayson and his gold-digging wife to hoodwink them into surrendering the deeds to them. The wife pretends to be the actual Mary Roberts and

feigns grief at the death of her father. 'What did he die of?' she asks tearfully to which Stan replies, thoughtfully, 'I think he died of a Tuesday.' The film, though, is justly remembered for the team's rendering of the song, 'The Trail of the Lonesome Pine.' Here is a privileged moment in Laurel and Hardy, a rare moment of harmony, a momentary ideal of order (like that moment when Stan seems to have washed all the plates in *Helpmates* and piled them up without mishap) – a sense of order that Ollie, above all, seems always to be vainly seeking. Even in this song, the harmony does not last long. Stan swoops into an improbable bass voice that stops Ollie short. He attempts to restore harmony by tapping Stan on the head with a wooden hammer, only for Stan now to soar into the sphere of the soprano before collapsing in a heap at Ollie's feet.

The other features are more patchy and uneven. A number of them – *Fra Diavolo*

(1933), *Babes in Toyland* (1934), *The Bohemian Girl* (1936) – take their plots from operetta to give a musical comedy surround to the pair's antics. *Our Relations* (1936) has a plot that seems roughly inspired by Shakespeare's *Comedy of Errors*, in which Laurel and Hardy play not only themselves but their disreputable twin brothers. *A Chump at Oxford* (1940) has perhaps the most interesting idea, as a blow on the head to Stan produces a transformation of their relationship. Reviewing the film at the time, Graham Greene noted that 'Laurel here is given more opportunity for straight acting; instead of an American hobo sent to Oxford by a benefactor, he becomes Lord Paddington, an all-round athlete who disappeared years before.' As Laurel starts ordering Hardy about, it is easy to see the situation as not only an inversion of their screen relationship but as a kind of allegory of their working relationship – Laurel the brains telling Hardy what to do. Before the end, though, the status quo is restored, and they thankfully, even movingly, slip back into their familiar roles.

Flawed as the films are, there are still many inventive and memorable move-

ments and scenes. In *Blockheads* (1938), Stan Laurel is ordered to guard a trench towards the end of World War I. Years later he is still patrolling the trench, with cans of beans piled up behind him like a hill: no one has told him the war is over. Stan also has superb solo scenes in *The Bohemian Girl* and *Swiss Miss* (1938). In the first he is assigned by Ollie to transfer wine from a barrel through a pipe into the bottles: what happens when he has filled one bottle and is searching for another while the pipe is still

ABOVE AND LEFT: Two moments from *Babes in Toyland* (1934).

spurting wine? Stan puts the pipe in his mouth, becomes more and more befuddled and the routine gets completely out of control. In *Swiss Miss*, he has a long scene with a truculent St Bernard – a kind of canine Ollie Hardy – as he tries to prise a bottle of brandy from between the dog's teeth, a scene which ends with Stan's having to simulate snow-fall with chicken feathers to catch the dog off guard.

The great scene in *Swiss Miss*, though, is the one in which the two are required to transport a piano across a rope suspension bridge. Pianos are always full of hazards for Laurel and Hardy (see, for example, *The Music Box* and *Way Out West*). Their progress is further complicated by the fact that Stan is still sozzled from the brandy he has taken from the dog and that, unbeknown to Ollie, a gorilla at one stage appears on the rope behind him. Both piano and gorilla will eventually fall, but the gorilla

will turn up again at the end of the film, throwing its crutches after the retreating Stan and Ollie.

The creativity of Laurel and Hardy on screen had passed its peak by around 1940. They appeared in a number of features for Twentieth Century Fox between 1941 and 1945 – *A Haunting We Will Go* (1942), *Jitterbugs* (1943), and *Air Raid Wardens* (1943) among them – but they had little creative control over script or direction, and Stan always spoke bitterly of his experience at Fox. One collectors' item, *Zenobia* (alternative title: *Elephants Never Forget*), directed in 1939 by Gordon Douglas, had Ollie Hardy co-starring not with Stan but with Harry Langdon, which started rumors of the break-up of one partnership and the start of another. However, the reason for this pairing was simply that Hardy's contract had a few months longer to run than Laurel's and Hal Roach wanted to slip him into another film before it ran out. If Roach did nurture some idea of a new partnership, the reviews for the film probably scotched that. 'When Hardy's hat is flattened under an enormous hoof and he lifts it with the old expression of patient stifled fury,' wrote Graham Greene, 'we look sadly round for blinking twisting Laurel, and Zenobia the elephant is no substitute.'

For Greene, one of the secrets of Laurel and Hardy's success, which made them for him more agreeable than Chaplin, was their unpretentiousness. 'Their clowning is purer,' he said. 'They aren't out to better an unbetterable world; they've never wanted to play Hamlet.' For Hal Roach, as we have seen, the secret was that they were both equally funny, and that therefore every joke just had more potential for laughs. But their appeal undoubtedly went deeper than this.

They took incompetence to new levels of ingenuity. Nothing in life was so simple that Laurel and Hardy could not fail at it. In that sense, they were reassuring to an audience, for everyone could feel superior to them: no spectator was quite as hapless as the two muts on the screen. Yet this feeling of superiority was more akin to love than contempt. Why was this?

BELOW: *Our Relations*, in which they play dual roles.

Perhaps it was because there was a sense of Everyman about Laurel and Hardy. On the one hand, they were classic comedy stereotypes. Stan Laurel was the idiot boy, the perpetual child, eternally in the land of the literal (when he is asked to serve a salad 'undressed' in *From Soup to Nuts* he strips to his underpants) and never achieving more than a very basic linguistic competence (in *The Bohemian Girl*, he affects to tell somebody's fortune by saying that 'I see a long woman and a dark journey'). If Stan is the gormless child, Ollie Hardy is the know-all grown-up, whose adulthood is really only a front, for he is as much a gullible dupe

as Stan is a glassy-eyed dope. His self-importance cries out for retribution, and gets it. Pushing in front of Stan to hang up his coat on a nail in *Busy Bodies*, it is he who gets the water in his face from the pipe that the nail has gone through. If Chaplin is screen comedy's Hamlet, Ollie Hardy is its Falstaff.

Comedy is pain because comedy is about failure, and inadequacy, and Laurel and Hardy seemed to penetrate to the core of that. But even beyond that, audiences seemed to have responded to something else as well: the reality of their characters; and the resilience of their partnership.

BELOW: Adrift at sea with an escaped murderer: Laurel and Hardy in *Saps at Sea*.

LEFT: Anita Garvin, Hardy and Laurel in *From Soup to Nuts*, in which the two play waiters. Laurel's strange clothing derives from his understanding of Hardy's instruction to him to serve the salad 'undressed.'

BELOW: Gypsy camp in *The Bohemian Girl*.

'We had fun and we did a lot of crazy things in our pictures,' said Ollie, 'but we were always real.' The reality was enhanced by the use of their own names. It was also enhanced by their films' style, which tended to be undemonstrative, unflashy. There was none of the manic speeded-up motion of Sennett's Keystone films, nor much elaborate montage. The style took its cue from Ollie's stoicism and projected a kind of deadpan inevitability about the mayhem that was unfolding before the camera. It is a style that has sometimes been criticized for slowness. But there was an appropriateness to all this. Stan and Ollie never thought very quickly. A thought to Ollie, in particular, was an experience, not the cause of spontaneous illumination but of painstaking deliberation: the slowness was all part of the character's peculiarly patient masochism. Moreover, much of the humor derived from the fact that Ollie, in particular, would invariably think long and hard before doing anything, and *still* do it wrong. But the so-called 'slowness' was also part of their cinematic craftsmanship:

knowing when to allow time for a laugh (it took the Marx Brothers several films to master that). When you watch Ollie's reaction to Stan's eating of a hard-boiled egg in *County Hospital*, you see a comedian with an absolute mastery in knowing when to play the comedy to the camera and when to play the comedy to the other character (something which took Woody Allen half-a-dozen films to master).

But the ultimate key to their immortality has something to do with the partnership itself. Alternately stoical and truculent, patient and outraged, Hardy is an incompetent at more or less everything, and Laurel is at once his scapegoat and excuse for failure. Hardy has a veneer of gentility and aspirations of dignity that Laurel unwittingly but invariably frustrates. The Marx Brothers will puncture other people's dignity, but Ollie inadvertently punctures his own or has it accidentally punctured by Stan. 'Here's another fine mess you've got me into,' he says to Stan in *Going Bye Bye* (1934). Stan is both nemesis and necessary: in a way, Ollie's face-saving alibi of inadequacy. Together they represent the fallibility of friendship – a trouble shared is a trouble doubled in Laurel and Hardy – and, in that very vulnerability, they touch on our feelings of inferiority and fallibility. Yet the eternity of their comradeship makes the inevitability of failure, the certain knowledge of failed aspirations and life's disappointment, that much easier to bear.

Laurel and Hardy were to know their fair share of disappointment – the critical contempt for their later films, for example, the anti-climax of the later part of their careers. But television was to bring them to new audiences, and compilation films from Robert Youngson, such as *Laurel and Hardy's Laughing 20s* (1965) and *The Crazy World of Laurel and Hardy* (1966) – were popular in celebrating their achievement. Oliver Hardy died in 1957; Stan Laurel in 1965. To his biographer, John McCabe, Stan recalled one particular incident on their last tour of Britain in 1953, that brought home to him how the public had felt about the films. They had docked at Cobh in Ireland and news of their presence had spread to people on shore. As Stan remembered it:

'There were hundreds of boats blowing whistles and mobs and mobs of people screaming on the docks. We just couldn't understand what it was about. And then something happened that I can never forget. All the church bells in Cobh started to ring out our theme song, and Babe looked at me, and we cried. . . . Maybe people loved us and our pictures because we put so much love in them. I don't know. I'll never forget that day. Never.'

BOTTOM: A publicity shot of Laurel and Hardy.

BOTTOM: A publicity shot of Laurel and Hardy.

CHAPTER FIVE

W C Fields

The motto for Harold Lloyd's screen hero was: if at first you don't suceed, try, try again. Laurel and Hardy had a similar underlying refrain except, that however hard they tried, it would invariably come out wrong. But W C Fields had a variation all his own. 'If at first you don't suceed,' he said once in an interview, 'try, try again. Then quit – no use being a damn fool about it.' His ethic was crisply summarized when he opined that 'a thing worth having is a thing worth cheating for.' 'Is this a game of chance?' asks a newcomer to a poker game in *My Little Chickadee* (1940). 'Not the way I play it,' replies Fields, darkly.

W C Fields was the great misanthropist of the movies. Whereas Hollywood in its heyday was renowned for spreading sunshine and good cheer, Fields represented malice in wonderland. This was one of the main sources of his appeal, particularly for those tired of the false sentimentality of Tinseltown. Fields's was an authentic voice of asperity which was probably truer to what most people really felt. As his biographer Robert Lewis Taylor commented: 'Most people harbor a secret affection for anyone with a low opinion of humanity.' Fields's opinion was not simply low: it was positively subterranean. He hated; he distrusted; he cheated; he insulted.

It was a persona he elaborated in his movies. In *The Man on the Flying Trapeze* (1935), when asking for time off to attend his mother-in-law's funeral (he is actually planning to sneak off to play some golf), a sympathetic employer says: 'It must be hard to lose your mother-in-law.' 'Yes, it is,' agreed Fields, ruminatively, 'almost impossible, in fact.' He was famous for his on-screen hostility to children, notably towards child star Baby LeRoy, who tormented him in *It's a Gift* (1935), and whose orange juice was allegedly spiked by Fields with a liberal portion of gin. ('That kid's no trouper,' said Fields contemptuously when the child later felt too ill to continue with his role.) When asked whether he liked children, he replied: 'Only if they are properly cooked.'

What contributed to the sharp edge of Fields's comedy (as it does with a lot of great comedians) was the sense an audience had that, underneath all the humor, Fields was not really kidding. The grumpiness was genuine, and likely to produce not only waspish wit but outrageous behavior. To avoid the sentimentality of the season, he would send out his Christmas cards in July. He did not simply express his disapproval when his romantic partner, Carlotta Monti, sang in the shower: he lit a fire under the door. Given his social misanthropy, it is no surprise that he was dismissive of President Roosevelt's efforts in the 1930s to lift America from Depression. He described Roosevelt's New Deal as a 'raw deal' and proposed an alternative: 'instead of a New Deal, we want a new deck.'

'He was an isolated person,' said the actress Louise Brooks (always an astute observer of character) about Fields. 'As a young man he stretched out his hand to Beauty and Love and they thrust it away. Gradually he reduced reality to exclude all but his work, filling the gaps with alcohol . . . He was also a solitary person. Years of traveling alone around the world with his juggling act taught him the value of solitude, and the release it gave his mind.' Ms

Brooks is not the only commentator to suggest that Fields's dedicated disgruntlement at life was rooted in a turbulent childhood and his consequent endeavor to make it on his own. He did marry but it was a relatively short-lived affair, the couple being divorced after seven years. One unresolved bone of contention between them, apparently, had been Fields's insistence on practicing his juggling act at the dinner table.

He was born William Claude Dukinfield in 1880, son of an Englishman who had emigrated to Philadelphia and who sold fruit and vegetables from a pushcart. Fields claimed he went into showbusiness because he was innately lazy as a child and it seemed a better alternative to finding a proper job. He discovered a natural aptitude for juggling at the age of nine (similar to his proud boast in *The Bank Dick* that 'I never smoked a cigarette 'til I was nine'), and left home at the age of 11 after a violent disagreement with his father. During the next few months he lived homeless on the verge of starvation, compelled to steal food to stay alive. He spent several nights in jail and was frequently beaten up in street

BELOW: W C Fields and Alison Skipworth in *If I Had a Million* (1932).

brawls. It was from these beatings, and not from drink, that Fields claimed he acquired one of his most distinctive features, his bulbous, ruddy, misshapen nose, which Kenneth Tynan was to describe as 'resembling a doughnut pickled in vinegar or an eroded squash ball.' 'There's something big about you,' says the hostile waitress to him in *Never Give a Sucker an Even Break* (1941), 'your nose.' The other thing he acquired from this particular period was probably his subsequent outlook on life. 'He came up the hard way and it made him bitter,' said the great Hollywood director Joseph L Mankiewicz, who co-scripted one of Fields's earliest talkies, *Million Dollar Legs* (1932). Mankiewicz recalled Fields as 'a horror . . . in some ways, one of the meanest human beings who ever lived.'

Fields began his professional career at the age of 11 as a juggler at a summer park in Philadelphia. He moved on to Atlantic City where he said they developed a good ruse for attracting an audience. 'One of the performers would go out in the surf,' he said, 'pretend to be caught in the undertow and shout for help. We would all be ready, rush in the water and drag the rescued per-

ABOVE: Fields and Alison Skipworth in *If I Had a Million*.

son into the performing pavilion. Naturally the crowd followed, and if it was a woman we rescued the crowd was particularly large. Once inside they bought drinks and we were supposed to be entertaining enough to keep them there. It was a great racket . . .' He also devised a method of dealing with any heckler in the audience. He appealed to the others in the audience not to be too hard on the heckler: it had happened to Fields once before, he told them, but after he had berated the annoyer from the stage, he felt terrible when 'the keeper of an insane asylum had come down the aisle and taken the poor chap out and back to the institution.'

By the age of 20, Fields had become a star in vaudeville. He made a prestigious European tour in 1901, appearing at the Folies Bergères and even doing a command performance at Buckingham Palace. This experience was to stand him in good stead for the movies. Like Chaplin, Keaton, and Langdon – and also subsequently, classic comics like the Marx Brothers, Eddy Cantor and Will Rogers – Fields had honed his talent in vaudeville which gave him two

LEFT: Blowing the froth off his ice-cream soda in *Never Give a Sucker an Even Break*.

ABOVE: Peggy Hopkins and W C Fields in *International House.*

RIGHT: Drinking and driving: W C Fields.

FAR RIGHT: Fields in *International House.*

particular advantages when he was to step before a movie camera. The first was that his comic character and his comic technique were more or less all in place by the time he came to perform for the movies: he was not searching for an image or a style. (Like all the greats, though, he was a real perfectionist, continually refining his approach. Joining Fields at Paramount at the request of Mack Sennett in the early 1930s, Bing Crosby was to marvel at how hard Fields worked for the effect of apparent spontaneity.) The second advantage of his vaudeville experience – and it was something that Chaplin and the Marx Brothers, for example, also exploited – was that it provided him with a rich repertoire of ready routines, tried and tested in front of live audiences, that could be simply transplanted to the movies. Indeed, his first film, the silent short, *Pool Sharks* (1915), was simply the filming of a comedy billiards routine he had developed and perfected in his act on stage.

Fields's film career was to start in earnest after his triumph on Broadway in 1923 in the role of Professor Eustace McGargle in the play *Poppy*. He was invited to repeat the role in a film version, now entitled *Sally of the Sawdust* (1925), and directed by the legendary D W Griffith, then past his prime, alas. He worked with Griffith again on *That Royle Girl* (1926) and, although neither film was memorable, Fields cherished the association and was always looking for another chance of collaboration. As late as 1943, he was writing to Griffith to say how much he would like Griffith to direct him as Pickwick in a film of *The Pickwick Papers* – a mouth-watering prospect that, unfortunately, never came to fruition.

Fields's film work in the late 1920s has been understandably overshadowed by his work in the following decade, when talkies had begun. Even that most eloquent of champions of silent comedy, James Agee, had to concede that Fields was the one great comedian of the talkies 'who could not possibly have worked so well in silence.' Yet his films of the late 1920s have a great deal of interest. In *Running Wild*, (1927), for example, he has a scene in which he goes in to ask for a raise and which Pare Lorentz described as 'one of the finest and most poignant characterizations I have

ever seen on the screen.' 'Poignancy' and 'characterization' are not things immediately associated with Fields, who would generally be regarded as a stone-hearted scoundrel playing limited variations on himself. Yet a performance like this anticipates what was to be one of Fields's greatest and most unexpected triumphs in films – his portrayal of Mr Micawber in George Cukor's film of *David Copperfield* (1935).

Running Wild was one of two films Fields made for director Gregory La Cava, the other being *So's Your Old Man* (1926). La Cava was subsequently to direct two of the classic Hollywood comedies of the 1930s, *My Man Godfrey* (1936) and *Stage Door* (1937), and was also to become one of Fields's closest friends. 'Next to my own,' Fields said about him, 'he has the finest comedy mind in pictures.' It was La Cava who gave Fields a very important piece of advice about the definition and development of his comedy style and personality. 'You're not a natural comedian, Bill,' he told him. 'You're a counter-puncher. You're the greatest straight man who ever lived. It's a mistake for you ever to do

ABOVE: Fields as Micawber and Freddie Bartholomew as David in George Cukor's film of *David Copperfield*.

RIGHT: Freddie Bartholomew (left), W C Fields (center) and Jean Cadell (right) in *David Copperfield*.

ABOVE: Sweet nothings:
Mae West and W C
Fields in *My Little
Chickadee*.

the leading. When you start to bawl and ham around and trip over things, you're pushing. I hate to see it.' It was valuable advice and in the future and at his best, Fields was, as Kenneth Tynan put it, to play 'straight man to a malevolent universe which had singled him out for destruction.'

Something of this later persona is prefigured in a film like *The Potters* (1927), in which Fields played the hen-pecked head of a family who, through a quirk of fate, became rich. It is a basic plot device that was to be the slender narrative thread of his two greatest comedies, *It's A Gift* (1935) and *The Bank Dick* (1940). Plot was never very important in a Fields movie, and was given a satirical death-blow in the narrative absurdities of *Never Give a Sucker an Even Break*. But the important thing in this early film is the situation of Fields within the family, isolated and persecuted either by monstrous matriarchy or disrespectful siblings. It is within the family unit that he launches his most effective counter-attacks against domesticity, respectability, and small-town aspiration.

But if ever a film comedian of this era needed sound, it was W C Fields. So much of his humor resided in that unique rasping voice as well as his elaborate linguistic confabulations. Only Fields could have kissed Mae West's fingers in *My Little Chickadee*, and then exclaimed: 'What symmetrical digits!' Both attributes, incidentally, were genuine articles in Fields. He did really talk like that and, according to his great friend and golfing companion, Oliver Hardy, had the gift of making anything seem funny simply through the way he used his voice. He was also an indefatigable reader of the dictionary and would use his findings sometimes when firing off irate letters to critics for bad reviews (for, whatever the

ABOVE: Uriah Heep (Roland Young) gets his come-uppance in *David Copperfield*. Fields is third from right.

RIGHT: Frank Lawton (left, as David Copperfield the young man), W C Fields (center, as Micawber) and Roland Young (right, as Uriah Heep) in *David Copperfield*.

outward casual appearance, he did really care about his work). 'Don't be a little schmuck all your life,' he wrote to Walter Winchell after the latter had savaged *My Little Chickadee* in a review in the *New York Daily Mirror*. 'Don't be like that cowardly fish of the jellyfish family (I'm a little rusty on my ichthyology and can't recall the name for the moment) which when it is frightened, runs and exudes a smelly, inky substance to cover up its trail.'

His early films of the sound era were relatively unmemorable. His first talkie was the two-reeler *The Golf Specialist* (1930) and during that year he made four shorts for Mack Sennett, *The Fatal Glass of Beer*, *The Pharmacist*, *The Dentist* and *The Barber Shop*. He appeared as Humpty Dumpty in an eccentric early Hollywood version of *Alice in Wonderland* (1933), though the best of his early sound comedies was probably his début film for Paramount, *Million Dollar Legs* (1932). The film has some kinship with the Marx Brothers' comedy of roughly the same time for the same studio, *Duck Soup* (1933). In it, Fields plays the tyrannical president of the mythical kingdom of Klopstockia. 'Don't you think he's handsome, father?' says his daughter about her suitor, to which Fields drawls in reply: 'Yeah, but I'll fix that.' The suitor is later arrested and when the daughter seeks assurance from dad that the authorities will not harm her lover, Fields offers the following reassurance: 'Only for about two hours. Then they'll shoot him.' Joseph Mankiewicz recalled that, at this time, Fields's contract forbade him to drink, so Fields said he would play golf every morning instead. He neglected to mention that his golf bags were actually packed with bottles of beer. His consumption of alcohol was to remain prodigious to the end of his life – two quarts of gin a day, plus wine and whisky –

128

but he was the least apologetic of drinkers. 'I was in love with a beautiful blonde once,' he tells his niece in *Never Give a Sucker an Even Break*. 'She drove me to drink – it's the one thing I'm indebted to her for.'

However, it was a Dickensian characterization that provided Fields with his first highly acclaimed part in sound films – that of Micawber in *David Copperfield*. Charles Laughton had originally been assigned to the role, but director George Cukor thought Laughton a little too sly for the part, lacking the character's essential innocence. He plumped instead for Fields. 'He was really born to play it,' said Cukor, 'even though he'd never played a real character role before – that rare combination of the personality and the part.' Unusually, Cukor found Fields charming to work with – more often Fields gave his directors a hard time – and full of suggestions and ad-libs that were always in character. It was Fields's idea to have a cup of tea on Micawber's desk so that when the character becomes agitated, Fields could colorfully convey his agitation by dipping his pen in his tea rather than the inkwell. It was Fields too who had the idea of providing Micawber with a wastepaper basket, thereby giving the actor a bit of comedy business when he gets his foot stuck. Ever one to encourage his actors to use their own imagination and instincts, Cukor was more than ready to listen to Fields's ideas and was flatteringly receptive which was no doubt partly the reason for their good relationship. Physically Fields was not ideal casting for the part, Cukor conceded, but, he said, 'his spirit was perfect.'

If *David Copperfield* was Fields's finest dramatic achievement in movies, the film that demonstrated his comic spirit at its most inspired is probably *It's A Gift*, directed by Norman Z McLeod in 1935. James Agee was to rank this and *The Bank Dick* as 'among the best comedies (and best movies) ever made.' More unexpectedly,

ABOVE: W C Fields and Jack Oakie in *Million Dollar Legs* (1932).

but very perceptively, he was to compare its portrayal of 'rabbity white-collar life' with that in the thriller *Shadow of a Doubt* (1943), scripted by Thornton Wilder for another mordantly misanthropic movie master, Alfred Hitchcock. What the two films unexpectedly share is an essentially subversive attitude to their boringly complacent communities, which in Hitchcock takes the form of revealing the monstrousness within and which, in W C Fields, takes the form of anarchic destruction. Fields is in his element. He is the hen-pecked head of a household really ruled by a bullying matriarch, marvelously played by Kathleen Howard. His children seem to exist only in order to complicate his simplest household tasks, making shaving in the bathroom not only difficult but hazardous; making progress across the floor positively dangerous ('Suffering sciatica!' Fields exclaims, as he slips on his son's roller-

skate); and making breakfast at the table crowded to the point of claustrophobia as his space is invaded and he cannot reach the things he wants.

Later he is even driven out of his own bedroom by his wife. 'Sweet repose,' he intones, as he prepares to sleep out on the verandah. At which point his seat collapses; the milkman arrives with his bottles insistently clanking in the crate; a coconut rolls down a fire escape like a rampaging squirrel; a clothes line is extended and squeaks like a mouse; and a shotgun goes off. If this were not enough, he is visited by an insurance salesman who insists on spelling out his name 'Karl LaFonge' and starts on his patter until chased away by Fields with a meat cleaver. The ultimate indignity occurs when Baby Dunk (played by the immortal Baby LeRoy) starts dropping things on the sleeping Fields through a hole in the upstairs porch, landing a grape

ABOVE: From left to right: Virginia Weidler, Zasu Pitts, W C Fields, Pauline Lord and Evelyn Venable in *Mrs Wiggs of the Cabbage Patch* (1934).

LEFT: W C Fields with Zasu Pitts in *Mrs Wiggs of the Cabbage Patch*.

ABOVE: 'Closed on account of Molasses': Fields shuts up shop in *It's A Gift*.

RIGHT: A feather in his cap. Fields in *The Bank Dick*.

FAR RIGHT: Fields in uniform: *The Bank Dick*.

right on his nose, and then in his mouth ('Shades of Bacchus!' Fields exclaims). However, when he takes to lobbing an ice-pick, Fields's passivity snaps. 'Even a worm will turn!' he says, making after the boy.

This superb set-piece is preceded by an even more inventive one. Presiding over his general store, Fields is awaiting the arrival of a truculent, near-deaf, totally blind customer, Mr Muckle (played by Charles Sellon), who blithely disregards Fields's exhortations to leave things alone and proceeds to dismember the store. 'Who is that man?' asks a customer, in horror and bewilderment, to which Fields replies calmly: 'He's the house detective.' Small wonder Fields is dreaming of escape and his own orange grove in California, particularly when a jar of molasses is split in his store ('the spreading-est stuff I ever saw!' he exclaims) and he has to shut down for the day, posting the notice: 'Closed on account of Molasses.'

He and the family head for California. There is another classic scene where they have a picnic on private property and, in no time at all, have buried the grounds in their

debris, particularly caused when Fields has been attacked by a dog which has shredded a pillow. 'Those are my mother's feathers!' wails his wife, to which Fields replies, bemusedly: 'I never knew your mother had any feathers.' As they are chased from the grounds, Fields, in their getaway, knocks over a statue of Venus de Milo. He defends himself with the explanation that 'she ran right in front of the car.'

Fields's screen character is at its finest and funniest in this film. His name in the film is 'Bissonette' but he insists on the pronunciation, 'Bisson-ay.' It is a mark of Fields's aspirations to aristocracy, pretensions of gentility that are just asking to be punctured. It is also a mark of his linguistic punctiliousness. Fields was a great juggler of language as well as other things and a master of the grandiloquent phrase. He would invariably refer to his most prominent facial feature as his 'proboscis': a nose by any other name would not sound as sweet. Typically, too, in this film, he mutters to himself, a sort of private communion. It is a recognition that a hostile world is not listening to what he is saying – Fields's characteristic gesture toward this world is an arm flung up defensively as if to ward off a blow. It is also a recognition that the company he prefers is his own. Of all the classic comedians, Fields is probably the most isolated, the most self-enclosed. 'I want to be alone,' says Oliver Hardy at the end of *Helpmates* as he sits in the shell of a house that Stan Laurel, in his friendly desire to light a welcoming fire, has inadvertently burnt to the ground. But Ollie can't live without Stan: W C Fields would prefer to live without anyone. He does not accommodate himself to the world, or challenge it, or even try to master it. As far as possible he wards it off.

If *It's A Gift* is not Fields's finest film, its only rival is *The Bank Dick*, directed in 1940 by Edward Cline from a screenplay by one Mahatma Kane Jeeves, which is one of W C Fields's more florid pseudonyms (he is credited for the story of *Never Give a Sucker an Even Break* under the name of Otis J Criblecoblis). The film is framed by a classic portrait of Fieldsian family life, which barely stops short of open warfare. He puts IOUs in his children's piggy banks and is assailed on all sides by his vengeful wife and children. 'Shall I bounce a rock off his

ABOVE: Success comes to the Sousé household: *The Bank Dick*.

RIGHT: Transformation to gentility: the ending of *The Bank Dick*.

head?' says his daughter, to which his wife replies: 'Show respect for your father, darling – what kind of a rock?' When introduced to his eldest daughter's fiancé, Og Ogilvy, his only real comment is on the man's name: 'Sounds like a bubble in a bubblebath.' Fields's name in this film is Egbert Sousé, and he does attain a measure of gentility at the end when the family come into a lot of money after he has sold a story to the movies. The transformation of the family at the end – now very prim, proper, and polite – is as hilariously exaggerated as their anarchic disrespect at the beginning. It is in essence a send-up of the American Dream, a subversive hymn to success without effort. It is an anti-Harold Lloyd movie.

Between the scenes of family life are two main plot-lines, neither of which is given a lot of attention. The more important involves Fields's inadvertent foiling of a bank robbery planned by Loudmouth McNasty and Repulsive Rogan, which leads to his employment as the bank detective. Apprehending a child with a toy pistol and enquiring darkly whether the weapon is loaded, Fields is told by the child's irate mother: 'Certainly not, but I think you are.' Complications ensue when a J Pinkerton Snoopington (the infallible Franklin Pangborn) arrives to inspect the bank's finances, which are in disarray because Ogilvy, who works at the bank, has been encouraged by Fields to invest in a very dubious mine. 'Has Michael Finn been in today?' says Fields to his barman, encouraging him to slip a lethal substance into Snoopington's drink, but all is resolved happily.

There is also a subplot about Sousé's directing a film. 'Godfrey Daniel! Mother of pearl!' exclaims Fields when his younger daughter hits him over the head with a megaphone, disturbing his concentration while lining up a scene. He has temporarily taken over from the actual director, one A Pismo Clam, who has collapsed in a drunken stupor, but he shows some deficiencies of tact when directing his cast: for example, his enquiry of a small actress,

LEFT: The bartender watches bemusedly as Fields absent-mindedly blows the head off his ice-cream soda. From *Never Give a Sucker an Even Break*.

BELOW: W C Fields in *The Man on the Flying Trapeze* (1935).

ABOVE: Master of ping pong: W C Fields in *You Can't Cheat an Honest Man* (1939).

'She standing in a hole?' 'Can't get the celluloid out of my blood!' exclaims Fields and, within the film's loose, mad structure, Fields creates room for a light satire on the movie business.

His most elaborate movie satire, though, is *Never Give a Sucker an Even Break*, directed in 1941 by Edward Cline from a story by Fields which he claimed to have written on the back of an envelope while sitting on the toilet. It mainly involves Fields narrating (and the film visualizing) a plot-less, continuity-less film to an increasingly irritated studio head, Mr Penguin (Franklin Pangborn), whose day started badly anyway when he entered the studio and was caught up in a parade of Nazi troopers.

In its surreal moments, the film is superb. When his bottle of whisky falls out of a plane window, Fields dives after it, his niece following. The two fall 2000 feet, though Fields's advice is encouraging: 'Don't worry about the first 1999 feet, dear . . . it's the last foot you have to be careful of.' He lands on a strange planet near a beautiful girl who has never seen a man, but his opportunity is thwarted by the arrival of her mother, Mrs Hemogloben (Margaret Dumont), with a hound that has two vampire teeth. He transfers his atten-

tion to the mother, and W C Fields's courtship of Margaret Dumont is a sight to behold.

Unfortunately, as happened with Laurel and Hardy and the Marx Brothers, he was surrounded by musical numbers, which are not quite satirical enough to be diverting rather than distracting. He was also given a singing niece (Gloria Jean) to spell out to an audience how lovable her uncle is. The film's playing with movie conventions, its self-conscious preposterousness as a comment on the preposterousness of films that take themselves seriously, looks ahead in a way to the madcap structures of a film-maker like Mel Brooks on movies like *Blazing Saddles* (1974) and *Young Frankenstein* (1974). But the sentimental concessions are a little wearing. Fields is at his best in this film when annihilating narrative structure and movie realism, and justifies the critic Robert Sklar's description of him as 'the supreme nihilist of sound comedy.' It is a pity that the film also wants him to be someone's favorite uncle.

There is still one wonderful scene, which is essential Fields, when he trades insults with a waitress at the studio canteen. Fields

RIGHT: W C Fields, with Dorothy Lamour (left), Martha Raye (above) and Shirley Ross (right) in *The Big Broadcast of 1938*.

LEFT: Fields does a ventriloquist act with his dummy Oliver in *You Can't Cheat an Honest Man*.

was a master of the oblique brickbat. He will not complain overtly of the toughness of the steak he had last week, but he will comment that 'I didn't see that old horse that used to be tethered outside here.' In criticizing the efficiency and hospitality of the waitress service, he will say only: 'If anybody comes in here and gives you a ten-dollar tip, scrutinize it carefully, because there's a lot of counterfeit money going around.' When ice is dropped unceremoniously into his lap, he will react merely by saying: 'No extra charge for the cold shower, I hope.' 'Good morning, *beautiful*,' he says to the glowering waitress and his farewell, after the hostilities of the meal, is, 'Thanks a thousand times.' Quick on the deadly drawl, absolutely controlled in his comic counterpunching, Fields's greatness and inimitability as a comedian could be

demonstrated from this scene alone.

Nevertheless after *Never Give a Sucker an Even Break* it is difficult to see where Fields's film career could have gone, for the movie industry is reduced to such absurdity here that one senses that Fields's filmic subversiveness is all but played out. There is a lovely moment, for example, when the all-important story conference is interrupted by a cleaner on her rounds, and further interrupted when she gets a phone-call on Mr Penguin's own phone. Picking up her bristly brush, Fields says, 'Take that Groucho Marx out of here, please.'

His co-starring venture with Mae West, *My Little Chickadee* (1940), had been something of an anti-climax. Both of them were a bit becalmed by the censor. Fields had a furious correspondence with Joe Breen at the Hays office who insisted that the line 'I

BELOW: Fields demonstrates how to ward off an Indian attack in *My Little Chickadee.*

know what I'll do, I'll go to India and become a missionary. I hear there's good money in it too' should be omitted for fear of offending religious sensibilities. Fields wrote that he was 'still prepared to sacrifice a valuable part of my anatomy to keep the line in,' but conceded that there was probably nothing he could do. 'Will this also have to be deleted from the European version,' he nevertheless persisted, 'or does that not come under your jurisdiction? I've

got to get a laugh out of this picture somewhere, even if it's down in India.' His later films, such as *Follow the Boys* (1944), where he repeats his pool-table routine, were mainly cameo roles.

'Any man who hates small dogs and children,' said the humorist Leo Rosten once of Fields, 'cannot be all bad.' Undoubtedly part of Fields's appeal was this element of hatred. He had a sacrilegious attitude to sentimentality and, for many, he therefore gleefully cut through the more glutinous elements of Americana: the reverence for family life, respectability, womanhood, heroism, and honesty. Fields, by contrast, was a scoundrel. He not only indulged his vices, but glorified in them, and even boasted of disreputable activities that he had not actually performed. When the bartender contradicts Fields's claim that he knocked down Waterfront Nell in *My Little Chickadee* and says that *he* did that, Fields responds somewhat huffily, 'Well, I started *kicking* her first.'

Of modern screen actors, although Rod Steiger has impersonated Fields in the movie bio-pic, *W C Fields and Me* (1975), the closest to him in style is probably Walter Matthau, the rumpled reprobate grumbling his way across what he sees as a malevolent fate. But with Matthau, one feels this personality is simply a part that he plays. For Fields, such misanthropy and suspicion sprang from the well-springs (or, one might say, the distillery) of his being. His distrust and debunking of institutionalized man – the banker, the film producer, the administrator, the insurance executive, the financier – were funny because they were genuine. In real life, Fields had over 700 bank accounts across the country to guard against one of them absconding with all his money or going bankrupt. It is said that he did this after being mugged when carrying his wages, which, until then, he had insisted should be paid to him in gold. But at its root is a more general paranoia, and playwright Arthur Miller, recalling this trait of Fields when thinking of his own father, saw it as the act of a turn-of-the-century man still mistrustful of, and ill-at-ease in, the modern world. Fields kept the world at arm's length through his own home-spun philosophy. When a fat man in *Never Give a Sucker an Even Break* asks him for a cure for insomnia, he replies, 'Get plenty of sleep.' He kept the world at arm's length also with drink. 'Drown in a vat of whisky,' he muses in *Sucker*. 'Death – where is thy sting?' It was precisely that kind of drollness that for Fields took the sting out of death – and life.

'It's a funny old world – you're lucky to get out alive.' So said Fields after the ceiling of his Hollywood apartment had fallen in on his head, necessitating his final move to a sanatorium in 1946. By this time arthritis and liquor had taken their toll, and it was on Christmas Day of that year that 'the fellow in the red nightgown,' as he referred to death, was to call on him. One of his last visitors was the actor Thomas Mitchell, who was surprised to find him sitting up in bed reading the Bible. Putting the good book down, Fields explained: 'I'm looking for the loopholes.'

BELOW: W C Fields in *The Bank Dick*.

CHAPTER SIX

The Marx Brothers

THE MARX BROTHERS

Apparently when the Jewish agency in Palestine recommended calling a halt to Jewish terrorism, W C Fields commented: 'That'll mean the end of the Marx Brothers' career.' He was not only joking, but also shrewdly putting his finger on the essence of Marx Brothers' comedy – namely, its aggression. The Marx Brothers were the terrorists of screen comedy. Their targets were the university campus, grand opera, political diplomacy, and high society. They did more than poke fun at such exalted institutions; they launched a full frontal assault. Anything in a stuffed shirt or uniform – a lawyer, a businessman, or a ship's captain – was particularly prone to their verbal or physical assaults.

After Laurel and Hardy, the Marx Brothers were the next great comedy team of the cinema, and the first great comedy team of the sound era. But, unlike Laurel and Hardy, they were not lovable buffoons but naughty boys with minds that reacted like quicksilver along quite unpredictable lines. They believed that the best form of defense was attack. Cornered as a stowaway in *Monkey Business* (1931), Groucho suddenly turns on the Captain. 'Do you know who sneaked into my state-room at three o'clock this morning?' he demands,

and when the Captain says no, he replies: 'Nobody, and that's my complaint. I'm young, I want gaiety, laughter, ha-cha-cha . . .' Their lines (penned by such master humorists as S J Perelman, Morrie Ryskind, George S Kaufman, among others) often had a Lewis Carroll-like illogic and surrealism that endeared them to such literary high-brows as T S Eliot and James Joyce. (Thornton Wilder always claimed to have spotted a reference to the Marx Brothers in Joyce's eruditely impenetrable literary epic, *Finnegan's Wake*.) Moreoever they fired their dialogue like bullets, which suited the hectic film style of the 1930s. Humphrey Bogart was to learn a lot from Groucho in the art of dialogue delivery, as you can hear in his opening scene with Lauren Bacall in *The Big Sleep* (1946), where even she is sufficiently impressed to say that he ought to be giving lessons on how to be a comedian.

Originally there were five Marx Brothers. The eldest was Leonard (later to become Chico, 1886-1961), and he was followed by Adolph, later Arthur (that is, Harpo 1888-1964), Milton (Gummo, 1893-1977), Julius (Groucho, 1890-1977) and Herbert (Zeppo, 1901-79). Their father was a Jewish tailor, whom Groucho described as 'probably the worst tailor in New York,' principally because he never used a tape measure: he would outfit customers by

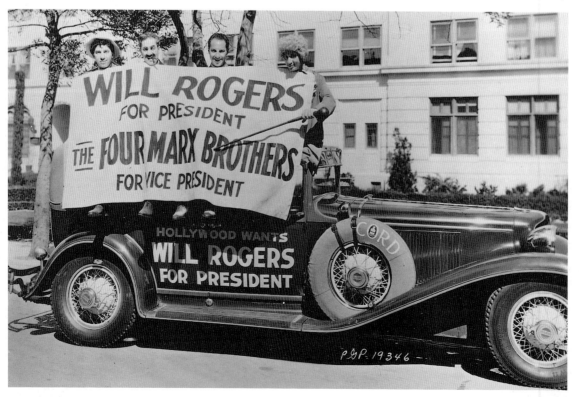

RIGHT: Chico, Groucho and Harpo in *A Night in Casablanca*.

LEFT: Paramount, 1930. On the campaign trail for Will Rogers, and themselves.

measuring them up by eye. But the real inspiration behind them was their mother,
Minna Schoenberg, who was the daughter
of show people and actively pushed her
boys toward the stage. Chico had had
piano lessons from the age of one, and indeed never lost the gift of being able to play
the piano like a one-year-old. Harpo taught
himself to play the harp and Groucho was a
boy singer. Indeed they started out as a
musical team, at that time led by Gummo
who, however, was to leave the act before
they achieved success, and was to be re-
placed by Zeppo.

Comedy came to them in an unexpected
way during a show in Texas, when half the
audience walked out in the middle of their
act to watch a mule on the rampage outside
the theater. When they came back,
Groucho changed the lyrics of the song to
insult the audience, and the boys rapidly
discovered that they were more popular
when sending up their own act than when
offering it straight. But they had to graft on
the vaudeville circuit for years before a
breakthrough. When they appeared at the
London Coliseum in 1922 under the stage

name of 'Herbert, Leonard and Julius' they
were booed off the stage. It was not until
1924 that they had a Broadway success with
I'll Say She Is!, and they followed it a year
later with an even bigger hit, *The Cocoanuts*.
When the sound era came to the cinema, so
did the opportunity of putting *The Cocoanuts* on film. Before this Harpo had
appeared in a silent movie called *Too Many
Kisses* (1925), an appearance so brief, he
said, that if you blinked, you missed it. But

TOP: Groucho, Margaret
Dumont, Chico and
Harpo in *A Night at the
Opera*.

ABOVE: 'The party of the
first part': Groucho and
Chico shred their
contracts, whilst Harpo
shreds Sig Ruman's
jacket. From *A Night at
the Opera*.

144

the sound era was made for the Marx Brothers, for language was their forte, although each had his own individual way of controlling it. Groucho masterfully manipulates it; Chico mischievously mangles it; Harpo manically mimes it. By this time, their comic characters were well established and developed, and were to become familiar and unmistakable over the next decade.

'Groucho,' says the critic Allen Eyles in an eloquent description, 'is the one whose visage is adorned by a crudely painted rectangle of a moustache, a pair of circular spectacle rims bereft of glass, eyebrows superciliating in a bizarre harmony with rolling eyeballs, and a mass of tangly hair that rises in pointed clumps from a central parting to give a touch of the devil. Add a stained frock-coat, uncreased pin-stripe trousers, and a pencil-thin tie as basic appendages to a body that is seriously bent half-way down but seems to progress all the faster for it.' Indeed this slinky, sidling walk seems an indispensible adjunct to Groucho's shiftiness and snaky cunning. He is the wit and cynic of the group. He can talk his way out of anything. Even more, he

can talk his way into anything. As the stowaway in *Monkey Business*, he even has the cheek to ring through to the bridge with the following calm instructions: 'Oh, engineer, will you tell 'em to stop the boat from rocking? I'm gonna have lunch.'

Groucho's quickness to take offense is matched only by his speed at giving it ('You're just wasting your breath and that's no great loss either'). He is something of a woman chaser but his line in romantic patter perhaps leaves something to be desired. For example, from *A Night in Casablanca* (1946): 'You're the most beautiful woman I've ever seen.' – 'Am I really?' – 'No, but I don't mind lying if it's going to get me some place.' When his romantic adversary is that great monument of straight-faced womanhood, Margaret Dumont, romance takes second place to the ironic insult. 'May I have a lock of your hair?' he asks her in *Duck Soup* (1933), before adding, 'I'm letting you off easy, I was going to ask for the whole wig.'

The only person who can frustrate and defeat Groucho linguistically is Chico who, in his gaberdine outfit and his basin-like hat, speaks his own brand of English in an

BELOW: Groucho watches as a bellboy tries to take the suitcase from the two guests, Chico and Harpo, in *The Cocoanuts.*

impossible Italian accent. In *Monkey Business*, having tried and failed to teach Chico the rudiments of Columbus's voyage, Groucho looks balefully at the camera and says, 'There's my argument. Restrict immigration.' He can be something of a rogue who occasionally even cons Groucho, notably during the tootsie-fruitsie routine in *A Day at the Races* (1937), where, as an ice-cream salesman, he persuades Groucho to buy numerous code-books to help him select a winning horse. Chico manages to select the winner, and Groucho is left with the ice-cream.

Chico often sits down to do an impromptu display on the piano, with a stiff index finger that runs along the keys in a manner all its own and, when asked by his audience what the first number is, he will generally reply, 'One.' Mainly, though, his most distinctive characteristic is his gift at mangling the English language, which makes communication very difficult (in *The Cocoanuts*, for example, when the word 'viaduct' has gone through Chico's linguistic mincer, it comes out as 'why a duck?'). When Chico is on trial for treason in *Duck*

Soup, Groucho summarizes his character as follows, 'He may talk like an idiot and look like an idiot, but don't let that fool you. He really is an idiot.' But the truth is more complicated than that and probably best indicated in the famous scene in *A Night at the Opera* (1935) when he and Groucho are drawing up a contract for his singer and slowly shredding it because of Chico's dissatisfaction. They are finally left with a thin strip of paper which Groucho explains is in

TOP: The four stowaways in the kippered herring barrels in *Monkey Business*.

ABOVE: Tormenting the captain in *Monkey Business*: Groucho, Ben Taggart, and Chico.

ABOVE: Zeppo, Thelma
Todd and Harpo in
Horse Feathers.

every contract – what they call 'a Sanity Clause.' 'Oh no, you can't fool me,' returns Chico. 'There ain't no Sanity Clause!'

Harpo Marx is perhaps the most complex of the three. He never speaks but can whistle or mime a message seemingly at the speed of light. His slapstick style, where he will suddenly prop his leg over someone's carelessly outstretched arm, is a cross between silent film comedy and surrealism. In *Horse Feathers* (1932), he quite literally unzips a banana and in *A Night at Casablanca*, when he walks away from a building on which he has been leaning, the building falls down. There is a Laurel-like literalness to Harpo, as in that moment in *Horse Feathers* when someone in a card game suggests that they 'cut the cards' and Harpo dutifully obliges – with an axe. The slapstick sometimes shows the influence of Chaplin in its use of mime, gesture and nimbleness of movement (which caused

W C Fields to liken Chaplin to a 'goddam ballet dancer'). Unlike Chaplin, there is no pathos in Harpo, but he is represented as woman-mad, constantly on heat, willing to take up the chase at the drop of a hat. He lusts at first sight. Chico's succinct explanation for Harpo's bizarre behavior is that 'he's half-goat.'

Of all the Marx Brothers, Harpo was the one whose screen character probably developed and changed most over the years, from 'idiot boy' to 'mute clown.' He would still communicate with gesture and carhorn but over the years the character became less ruthless, and alarming, more likeable and conventionally sympathetic. Of the other Marxes, Gummo was never to appear in any of the films, and Zeppo's last film with them was *Duck Soup*, after which he could no longer satisfy the studio bosses that he was what the boys needed in the way of a romantic lead. He even plays

Groucho's son in *Horse Feathers*, uttering such deathless questions as: 'Anything further, father?' Not even Groucho could swallow that line. '"Anything further, father?"' he echoes in disbelief. 'That can't be right. Shouldn't it be anything father further? The idea. I married your mother because I wanted children. Imagine my disappointment when you arrived.'

There is some dispute, even among the Marx Brothers themselves, about which period in films constituted their finest. Their early films, from *The Cocoanuts* in 1929 to *Duck Soup* in 1933, were made at Para-

mount. The first two films, *The Cocoanuts* and *Animal Crackers* (1930), set up the style of the more famous works to follow. In the earlier film, as the hotelier Mr Hammer, Groucho demonstrates his knack of disarming his opponent simply by turning his antagonist's line back on him, when the bellboys ask for their money. 'Oh – you want my money?' he says. 'Is that fair? Do I want *your* money?' In the same film he courts Margaret Dumont's Mrs Potter with dubious discretion. 'Your eyes, they shine like the pants of a blue serge suit,' he offers and when even she notices that this is an insult, he replies: 'That's not a reflection on you – it's on the pants.' He will later say she reminds him of the Prince of Wales. *Animal Crackers* is most memorable for its 'Hooray for Captain Spalding' song; Groucho's dictation to Zeppo of a letter to the law office firm of Hungerdunger, Hungerdunger, Hungerdunger and McCormack; its satire on the verbal asides of Eugene O'Neill's play, *Strange Interlude*; and a typical piece of Marx logic between Groucho and Chico where, stage by stage, they get to the point where they seem to be arguing that a stolen painting was eaten by left-handed moths.

In *Monkey Business* (1931) they play stowaways on an ocean liner who are first discovered singing 'Sweet Adeline' in some kippered-herring barrels. The boys become involved in protecting two sets of rival

ABOVE: Margaret Dumont, Groucho and Zeppo in *Animal Crackers*.

RIGHT: Chico and Harpo in conflict in *Animal Crackers.* Groucho and Margaret Dumont look on.

TOP: Harpo orders a drink in the speakeasy in *Horse Feathers*. With Groucho, Chico and Vince Barnett.

ABOVE: Game plan in *Horse Feathers*, though Harpo has a plan of his own.

bureaucracy to complete chaos, completing the mayhem by rubberstamping the customs officer's bald head.

Meanwhile Groucho has two scintillating passages of ego deflation. The first occurs when pretending to be a newspaper interviewer putting a variety of leading questions to a prima donna: 'Is it true you're getting a divorce as soon as your husband recovers his eyesight? Is it true you wash your hair in clam broth?' The second occasion is his introduction of a musical interlude, which will later feature the traditional piano solo from Chico and the harp solo from Harpo: 'I wish to announce that a buffet supper will be served in the next room in five minutes. In order to get you into that room quickly, Mrs Schmalhausen will sing a soprano solo in this room.'

Although the Marx Brothers' films invariably had musical interludes, it was characteristic of Groucho to keep the fun going by making some deprecatory remark. In their following film, *Horse Feathers* (1932), when the musical number is about to start, Groucho will turn to the camera

mobsters and it will end in a rather protracted fight in a barn, Zeppo fighting, Groucho watching. The film is mainly memorable for the first half on the ship, as they dodge and demoralize the ship's captain, and then try to sneak through the customs post by claiming to be Maurice Chevalier. Harpo's impersonation is the most elaborate, as he has a wind-up gramophone and record concealed behind his coat. Exhilaratingly, he reduces the

ABOVE: Groucho courts
Margaret Dumont in
Duck Soup.

nounced in the earlier films than in the later
ones, where music is incorporated far more
self-consciously, to lend the boys a more
romantic 'likeable' aura.

In *Horse Feathers* (1932), Groucho plays
the new Professor of Huxley College,
Quincy Adams Wagstaff, whose educa-
tional philosophy is expressed in a racy
production number entitled: 'Whatever it
is, I'm against it' (Groucho's screen credo
in a nutshell). He becomes involved with
the 'college widow' (Thelma Todd), who is
in league with a heavy who is attempting to
find out Huxley's football signals to ensure
that the rival college Darwin can win the
game so he can collect on the bet. 'This is
the first time I've been out in a canoe since I
saw *An American Tragedy*,' purrs Groucho,
and when the lady coquettishly suggests
that he is 'full of whimsy' he replies: 'Can
you notice it from there? I'm always that
way after I eat radishes.' The game will be
saved by some spectacular work in particular by Harpo, who first satirizes *Ben Hur* by
arriving at the ground using a garbage cart
as a chariot, and then mimics Harold Lloyd
in his madcap antics on the football field,
upending his opponents by judiciously
dropping banana skins on the turf.

Their next film, *Duck Soup* (1933),
directed by Leo McCarey (undoubtedly the
best director they ever worked for) is Marx
humor at its most savage and surreal and is
without doubt one of the classics of
American screen comedy. Watching this
film is the thing that saved Woody Allen's
character from suicide in *Hannah and Her
Sisters* (1986). It has the best visual routine
of any Marx Brothers film, with Chico and
Harpo both disguised as Groucho in an
identical ghostly white nightgown, finally
encountering both each other and the real
thing in front of a broken looking glass,
which results in a fantastic prolonged
mime that is essentially a battle of wits between 'reality' and its 'reflexion.' *Groucho
through the Looking Glass* it could be called,
for it has the weird logic and bizarre imagination of a Lewis Carroll. But else-
where, too, the film contains the best of
Groucho wit, of Chico cunning, of Harpo
hilarity, and coursing through it too is a
political satire of a wit and savagery unmatched in the American cinema probably
until Kubrick's *Dr Strangelove* (1964).

It is a film that mocks political states-

and say: 'Listen I have to stay here, but
why don't you folks go out to the lobby for
a smoke until this thing blows over?' It is a
very interesting moment. It is almost a premonition of that screen character in Woody
Allen's *The Purple Rose of Cairo* (1985) feeling
imprisoned within his screen role and
rather wishing he was part of the audience
rather than part of the film. Equally striking
is the fact that Groucho's sending up of
these musical numbers is more pro-

RIGHT: Chico and Harpo inform an unimpressed Louis Calhern of their spying activities in *Duck Soup*.

BELOW: Treachery afoot: Groucho and Margaret Dumont suspect a plot against Freedonia in *Duck Soup*.

manship. 'If you think this country's bad just now, just wait 'til I get through with it,' sings Groucho as Rufus T Firefly, now ruler of Freedonia, largely through the patronage of Mrs Teasdale (Margaret Dumont) who holds the nation's purse-strings. 'O your Excellency!' she enthuses to Firefly, to which he replies: 'You're not so bad yourself.' Needless to say, Firefly turns out to be a paragon of political venality and ineptitude. He is romantically unscrupulous, quickly moving in on Mrs Teasdale when he discovers that her husband is dead: 'Will you marry me? Did he leave you any money? Answer the second question first.' He is politically undiplomatic, to say the least, approaching the Ambassador of Sylvania (Louis Calhern) with the words: 'Now, how about lending this country twenty million dollars, you old skinflint?' His cabinet meetings are spectacularly non-productive, partly because of his own incomprehension ('A four-year-old child could understand this report. Run out and find me a four-year-old child. I can't make head or tail of it'), but mainly because of his political ruthlessness, or 'Rufusness' as he

would call it (to the workers' demand for shorter hours, he responds by 'giving them shorter hours. We'll start by cutting their lunch hour to twenty minutes'). Add to this a prickly temperament that can see an insult behind every greeting ('The man doesn't live who can call a Firefly an upstart. Why the Mayflower was full of Fireflys, and a few horseflies too') and it is inevitable that the country will soon be plunged into war. 'Go, and never darken

my towels again,' he says imperiously to the Sylvanian Ambassador and readies himself for conflict. During the subsequent battle, the Secretary (Zeppo Marx) will have to point out to him that he is actually shooting his own men.

While Groucho is constructing one of the cinema's most iconoclastic portraits of political power – soon to be matched by Chaplin in *The Great Dictator* – Chico and Harpo are also at their most impish, playing the

ABOVE: Groucho informs Margaret Dumont of his plans to get her into high society in *A Night at the Opera*.

Sylvanian Ambassador's spies, Chicolini and Pinky. Chicolini completely bamboozles the Ambassador with his account of his shadowing of Firefly: 'Monday we watch Firefly's house, but he no come out. He wasn't home. Tuesday we go to the ball game, but he fool us. He no show up. Wednesday he go to the ball game and we fool him. We no show up. Thursday was a double-header. Nobody show up.' Meanwhile Pinky has been building up a rivalry with a lemonade salesman (Edgar Kennedy) outside the presidential palace, a rivalry that will end with his clambering through Kennedy's lemonade in his bare feet to discourage sales. Chicolini and Pinky will eventually wind up in the employ of Firefly in the War Department.

Some of the routines and gags of the film had first been aired on the Marx Brothers' radio series, *Flywheel, Shyster and Flywheel*, but this hardly matters: the script by Bert Kalmar, Harry Ruby, Arthur Scheckman and Nat Perrin is quite brilliant. So too is an extraordinary production number when war is declared and the court bursts into the song, 'All God's chillun' got guns,' the Marx Brothers doing a happy xylophone cadenza on the soldiers' helmets. It is at moments like these when one sees what commentators mean when they talk of the element of subversiveness and danger inherent in great comedy, for beneath the riotous humor here is a disturbing comment on political and human aggression, the ease with which war-like emotional fervor can be fanned and inflamed. The fact that what they are fighting for – 'Remember that you're fighting for this woman's honor, which is probably more than she ever did' – might not be worth the candle is another disturbing undertone, for how many wars are really fought for the noble motives ascribed to them?

ABOVE: Harpo entertains the children in *A Night at the Opera.*

RIGHT: Harpo and Chico run riot in the orchestra pit in *A Night at the Opera.*

Assuredly the most brilliant of the Marx Brothers' comedies, *Duck Soup* might also have been just too ruthless and cynical for the general audience. It was not a commercial success. With the darkening political situation in Europe, it could be that its comical truths about greed and ambition in high places were a little too close to the bone: the more accurate the satire, the more painfully it can seem to press on a sensitive nerve. It might have been a little too unrelenting and intellectual for popular taste. There is no romantic subplot (one can hardly count Firefly's reverie about mar-

'Monroe Stahr' and played by Robert DeNiro in the 1976 film version). Thalberg startled the Marx Brothers at their first meeting by telling them that, in his view, they knew nothing about screen comedy. By toning down their aggressiveness, he felt he could make them more popular, especially to women in the audience. Their films should have contained more plot, more romance, more music, he thought, to broaden their appeal. Out of this came *A Night at the Opera*, (1935), which in a sense proved Thalberg right: it was a big critical and commercial success. It was also

RIGHT: Groucho disguises Harpo, Allan Jones and Chico as Russian aviators in *A Night at the Opera*.

riage to Mrs Teasdale: 'Married! I can see you right now in the kitchen bending over a hot stove, but I can't see the stove'). There are also no musical interludes for Chico's piano and Harpo's harp. It might also have been the victim of bad timing. Its hostility to politics came at a time when the country was responding to President Roosevelt's enlightened guidance and his exhortation of community harmony and teamwork to defeat the Depression. However dizzily and dazzlingly expressed, the message of *Duck Soup* was not the one the country at that time wanted to hear.

In any event, it turned out to be their last film for Paramount, and the last film of theirs in which Zeppo appeared. They now moved to MGM and were put under the stewardship of 'boy wonder' producer, Irving G Thalberg (soon to be immortalized in F Scott Fitzgerald's uncompleted last novel, *The Last Tycoon*, as the producer

Groucho's favorite of their films.

In it Groucho plays Otis B Driftwood who has been employed by Mrs Claypole (Margaret Dumont) to introduce her into high society. His scheme, which is less than zealously pursued, is to accomplish this by making her the patroness of the opera, after which, he says, all New York will be at her feet – 'and there's plenty of room.' Meanwhile, Chico and Harpo are helping the prima donna Rose (Kitty Carlisle) to fend off the attentions of the esteemed tenor Lasparri (Walter King) and encourage the singing ambitions of her true love, Ricardo (Allan Jones).

For those who like their Marxism served undiluted, the romantic sub-plot is a little obtrusive, as the film juggles with the problem of making the boys more sympathetic while at the same time retaining their comic cutting edge. For the most part it works, for the film – smoothly directed by Sam Wood,

and stylishly scripted by George S Kaufman and Morrie Ryskind – has some of their funniest set-pieces, notably a scene in which more and more people pile into Groucho's cabin and finally explode into the corridor when Margaret Dumont opens the door. The film's climactic highlight is the opera scene itself, in which the Marx Brothers launch their most sustained and irreverent assault on high culture. Their high-jinks ensure that Verdi's *Il Trovatore* is well and truly murdered; Groucho undercuts aesthetic enjoyment when he remarks to an opera buff about one straining soprano, 'How would you like to feel the way she looks?'; and Harpo simply brings the performance to a halt when, in one spectacular fall, he slits a theatrical backdrop clean down the middle. When giving full rein to the Marx Brothers' anarchic spirit, *A Night at the Opera* is a milestone of movie comedy.

Sadly, they would never reach such cinematic heights again. Groucho dated the decline from the moment when three weeks into the shooting of their next film, *A Day at the Races* (1937), they learnt that

LEFT: Chico and Harpo interrupt Groucho's love scene with Esther Muir in *A Day at the Races*, telling him that she's out to get him. 'Why, I've never been so insulted in my life,' says the lady, to which Groucho replies: 'Well, it's early yet.'

RIGHT: 'Get your tootsie-fruitsie ice-cream': Chico cons Groucho in *A Day at the Races*.

LEFT: 'This woman is mine!': the Marxes fight over Esther Muir in *A Day at the Races*.

RIGHT: Groucho in disguise tries to elude Chico and Harpo in *A Day at the Races*.

queried, assures everyone that 'the last patient I gave these to won the Kentucky Derby.' He also has a very funny seduction scene, which is constantly being interrupted by Chico and Harpo, who claim that his lady friend is in league with a man trying to discredit Groucho. 'Why, I've never been so insulted in my life!' cries the girl, to which Groucho responds: 'Well, it's early yet.' If the film feels a little heavy, the reason is that some of the comedy scenes fall a little flat. The 'tootsie-fruitsie' exchange between Chico and Groucho is not on the same level as their 'sanity clause' routine in *Night at the Opera*, and Allan Jones and Maureen O'Sullivan make relatively charmless romantic leads who occupy too much screen time.

None of the Marx Brothers' remaining films succeed as satisfying wholes. *Room Service* (1938) is well enough performed by them but is essentially uncharacteristic, a conventionally filmed stage piece not written with them specifically in mind. Buster Keaton was involved uncredited on the script of *At the Circus* (1939), though the story goes that Groucho and Keaton were at loggerheads, Groucho feeling that Keaton's humor was unsuitable for their films, Keaton feeling that Groucho was a thoroughly bad lot, even teaching his grandchild to cheat at cards (Keaton, along with Jack Benny and S J Perelman, always thought that Harpo was by far the nicest of

Thalberg had died at the age of 37. For Groucho, it left not only the film rudderless (and at 109 minutes, it is a little long and could have done with some sympathetic editing), but also without a guiding hand for their subsequent film career, for he had come to rely heavily on Thalberg's judgment. As Dr Hackenbush in *A Day at the Races*, Groucho is a horse-doctor appointed to head the Standish Sanitarium and who, when his prescription of a horse-pill is

the Marx Brothers). Nevertheless Groucho has the film's best moments, whether bidding farewell to the monkeys – 'Goodbye Mr Chimps' – or courting an old flame (Margaret Dumont), who does not remember him: 'We were young, gay, reckless. The night I drank champagne from your slipper – two quarts. It would have held more but you were wearing inner soles.' When told that 400 people have been invited to a society party of Dumont's, he insists on counting them all individually and concludes sadly that they have all showed up and that 'there'll be no second helpings.'

Go West (1940) is as disappointing a send-up of the Western as the W C Fields/Mae West co-starrer *My Little Chickadee* (1941), though there is a nice exchange of tough-guy dialogue, where Groucho asks, 'Say, where'd I see your face before?' to which Chico snarls in reply: 'Right where it is now.' *The Big Store* (1941) is chiefly memorable for one moment in which Groucho suddenly quotes the poetry of that great romantic of the early nineteenth century, Lord Byron, 'She walks in beauty like the night of cloudless climes and starry skies.' 'Why, that's Byron,' says Miss

LEFT: Harpo, Frank Albertson, Chico and Groucho in *Room Service*.

RIGHT: The human cannonball: Harpo, Groucho and Chico in *At the Circus*.

BELOW LEFT: Harpo (on the door), Chico and Nat Pendleton in *At the Circus*.

BELOW: Groucho seems doubtful about Harpo's beaver hat in *Go West*.

Dumont, impressed, to which Groucho snaps back in one of the most back-handed of all his compliments, 'He was thinking of you when he wrote it.'

Their first postwar film was *A Night in Casablanca*, directed by Archie Mayo in 1946. It has a hilarious fencing duel for Harpo, a nice piano solo for Chico ('Who's Sorry Now'), and a slapstick routine for the three of them, dodging around in the closets of Count Pfefferman (the incomparable Sig Ruman), that represents their neatest visual comedy for a decade. But nothing in the film is as funny or as memorable as the correspondence it precipitated between Groucho Marx and the Warner Brothers' Legal Department, who were worried that the film might be confused with their own big hit, *Casablanca*, and wanted a change of title. Groucho retorted by saying that most movie-goers could tell the difference between Harpo Marx and

ABOVE: Groucho and Margaret Dumont share a drink in *At the Circus*.

Ingrid Bergman; and, as for their claim that they own the title 'Casablanca' and no one else can use it, what, Groucho queried, about the company's use of the word 'Brothers' in Warner Brothers? ('Professionally, we were brothers long before you were.') Eventually the legal department backed off in some disarray and confusion.

Their last film together as a team was *Love Happy* (1949), which is remembered nowadays chiefly for an early screen appearance by Marilyn Monroe who tells private-eye Groucho that she thinks she is being followed. 'I can't think why,' says Groucho, his eyebrows working overtime.

Groucho was to become a nationwide celebrity in the 1950s through the popularity of his television show, *You Bet Your Life*; and something of a literary celebrity too after the publication of his letters to such eminent writers as T S Eliot ('Thank you for your photograph. I had no idea you were so handsome'), and to such organizations as a Hollywood club that had offered him membership, 'I don't care to belong to any social organization that will accept me as a member.' Harpo also published his memoirs, *Harpo Speaks*! in 1961, whilst Chico generally devoted his retirement to whisky and women. After the success of

RIGHT: Harpo, Chico, Virginia Grey and Groucho in *The Big Store.*

BELOW: Not to be confused with Bogart and Bergman: Harpo, Groucho and Chico in *A Night in Casablanca.*

Some like it Hot (1959) and during the period when the Cold War was at its frostiest, master director Billy Wilder attempted to reunite the Marxes for a film that let them loose in the United Nations. But Harpo had a heart attack, which made the Brothers uninsurable as a team for a major movie, and Wilder felt it would not work with anyone else.

At the end of *A Night in Casablanca* there is a madcap scene in which the brothers go crazy in an airplane, Harpo in particular flicking switch after switch and growing more manically happy as the danger looms ever larger. Symbolically, wondered the art critic Erwin Panofsky, is this scene really a comment on a modern technological age run riot, a theme at that time particularly potent after the dropping of the atomic bomb? It is tempting to read deep significance into the Marx Brothers' humor, and it is probably no coincidence that their films experienced a revival of popularity in the iconoclastic 1960s, for no one mocked authority and pomposity with greater panache.

As well as the social dimension of their comedy, there was also an air of the surreal, both verbally in their dialogue, and visually in their sight-gags (like the moment in *Duck Soup* when a live dog appears out of the drawing of a house on Harpo's chest – it is like something out of Luis Buñuel). At their best they were the supreme anarchists of screen comedy, defying logic and taste and unleashing a tonic madness at a grey world. When the Marx Brothers are in full flight, there ain't no sanity clause.

CONCLUSION

When Richard Burton was reluctant to co-star yet again with his wife, Elizabeth Taylor, he explained his misgivings as follows: 'Well we don't want to become another Laurel and Hardy.' 'Why?' replied Taylor, 'What's so bad about Laurel and Hardy?'

It is a good question. The cinema has always needed its Laurel and Hardy and when their film career faltered in the 1940s, it is interesting how a medley of comedy teams strove to take their place. For many observers, the strangest was the team of Bud Abbott and Lou Costello. 'A phenomenon of showbusiness,' said the critic Raymond Durgnat ironically about them, 'because they were totally devoid of any striking characteristic except that one is short and fat and the other tall and thin.'

They certainly never developed the kind of bond and characterization that marked the partnership of Laurel and Hardy, but they did have their own style and a kind of childish appeal. 'Throw your chest out!' says Bud to Lou in *Buck Privates* (1941) to which Lou replies, 'I'm not through with it yet.' When asked if he knows where the subconscious mind comes from (in *Abbot and Costello Meet the Invisible Man*, 1951) Lou replies, 'The subway.' Lou is the gag-man and the one whom the audience is meant to like for his childlike demeanor: even when a detective, he will suck his Sherlock Holmes-type magnifying glass as if it were a lollipop. By sticking to well-tried routines and not becoming too ambitious with their projects, they maintained a steady popularity.

RIGHT: Bud Abbott and Lou Costello as fledgling detectives in *Abbott and Costello Meet the Invisible Man* (1951).

BOTTOM RIGHT: Tasty morsels: Abbott and Costello in *Africa Screams* (1949).

BELOW: An early appearance of The Three Stooges in *Dancing Lady* (1933), with Joan Crawford and Ted Healy. From left to right the Stooges are Larry, Moe and Curly.

163

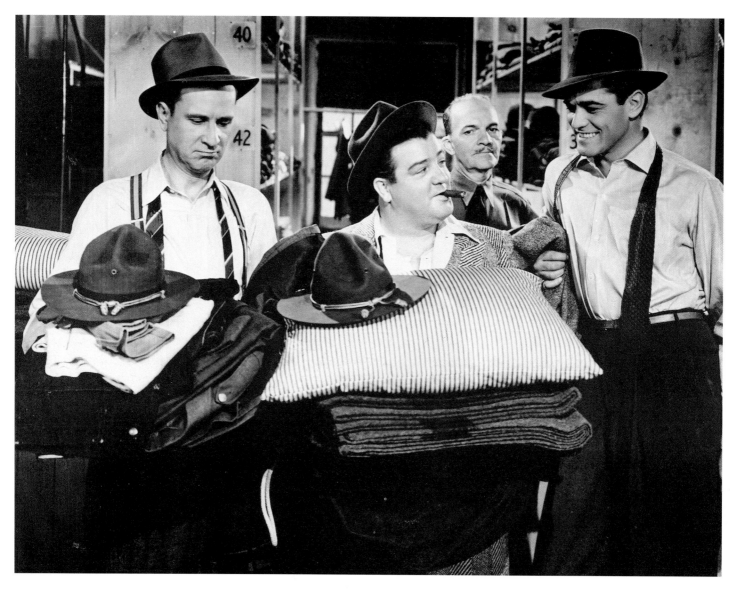

Another movie team, who sustained their popularity over 40 years and 200 films, irrespective of critical disdain, were the Three Stooges – Moe the stubborn one, Larry the blank one and Curly the agile, enthusiastic one. (Shemp Howard, who played the bartender in W C Fields's *The Bank Dick*, was later to replace Curly as the third Stooge when Curly suffered a stroke). Sometimes the titles of their movies – *Cactus Make Perfect, Calling All Curs, All the World's a Stooge, Phony Express* – were funnier and more imaginative than the films themselves. Yet some of their work does obstinately lodge in the memory, like their co-starring work opposite Clark Gable and Joan Crawford in *Dancing Lady* (1933), or their hospital spoof *Men in Black* (1934), a film that received their one and only Oscar nomination. In their first short, *Woman Haters* (1934), they deliver their dialogue entirely in verse; *Tassles in the Air* (1938),

directed by that fine silent comedian, Charley Chase, has them as very funny interior, and inferior, decorators; and *Three Little Beers* (1935) has some of their best sight gags where they take up golf and proceed to wreck the course, covering it with divots ('What are you complaining about? Don't you see they're getting smaller?' says Moe to the irate gardener) and chopping down a tree to retrieve a ball stuck in one of the branches. In *Cactus Makes Perfect* (1942) there is a memorable appearance by their mother, spinning them like a top to get them out of bed in the morning and, at one stage, managing to hit all three with one magisterial, matriarchal blow.

The common complaint about their humor, apart from its low vulgarity and childishness, was its violence. An exchange like the one between Moe and Curly in *Dizzy Pilots* (1943), when they are inventing a new airplane, is fairly typical.

164

ABOVE: The Three Stooges and lady friend in the golfing saga, *Three Little Beers* (1935).

LEFT: Hapless decorators in *Tassels in the Air* (1938).

'Where's your vice?' says Moe, to which Curley replies, 'I have no vice, I'm as pure as driven snow.' 'But you drifted,' says Moe contemptuously, incidentally stealing a Mae West gag ('I was Snow White – but I drifted'), and then slapping him. The Three Stooges represented the slapstick tradition in a very primitive form but one that maintained an undoubted appeal. When the Inspector in that same film watches their crazy aerial antics as the Stooges test their plane, he says: 'They're either miracle men – or insane.' A good evocation of their humor.

A classier act altogether was that of Bob Hope and Bing Crosby whose teaming on *Road to Singapore* (1940) was so successful that it led to a series of *Road* movies. Crosby's droll style was the perfect foil to Hope's wisecracking, and his romantic assurance sweetly complemented Hope's brittle swagger. In Hope's persona of the

sexual braggart, the devout coward, the man who uses wit to hide his insecurity, one can see many anticipations of the early Woody Allen. Allen clearly learnt a lot from Hope, in his send-up of cinematic conventions, his sly asides to the camera. 'If I wanted to have a weekend of pure pleasure,' said Allen, 'it would be to have a half-dozen Bob Hope films and watch them, films like *Monsieur Beaucaire* and *My Favorite Brunette*.' Allen dates his interest in comedy from seeing Hope in *Road to Morocco* in 1942 and has always thought him 'a great, great talent.'

As the *Road* films peaked in popularity, Hope and Crosby were then displaced by a more controversial partnership, Dean Martin and Jerry Lewis, who made 18 films together from *My Friend Irma* in 1949 to *Hollywood or Bust* in 1956 before Lewis went solo. Again Martin's coolness nicely complemented Lewis, but part of the fascination

RIGHT: Martin and Lewis in *You're Never Too Young* (1955), a remake of Billy Wilder's *The Major and the Minor* (coincidentally the actress Diana Lynn played in both versions).

ABOVE: Dueling cat and mouse: Tom and Jerry in *The Two Mouseketeers*.

of their teaming was its sheer incongruity; what was a smooth charmer like Martin doing with such a lunatic like Lewis? Had he spotted something in his character that we had missed? Could this mystifying marriage of mildness and mania last?

Jerry Lewis has remained something of a bone of contention between American and European critics and between aficionados of film comedy generally. That acute observer, Stan Laurel, thought he had 'much

talent' but not enough 'artistic discipline.' Lewis himself described his comic persona as a split personality between 'The Kid' and 'The Idiot,' in which the failure of the former's search for love turns him into the 'childish grotesque' of the latter – someone who hides behind a mask of clownishness, who retreats into fantasy. A film like Lewis's *The Nutty Professor* (1963) is his version of Jekyll and Hyde and a literal treatment of the 'split personality' theme. At his best as, say, a hospital orderly in *The Disorderly Orderly* (1965), he can seem wildly and exhilaratingly inventive while, at his worst, he can seem hysterical, childish, and sentimental. The sentimentality is much less acceptable than Chaplin's, because it lacks Chaplin's counterbalancing harshness and astringency and its rootedness in a sense of what humanity is up against. But he is a remarkable physical comedian – 'he thinks with his body,' commented the critic Raymond Durgnat astutely – with a full range of facial contortion, manic gallop, or limp posture to suggest a personality who is blocked and repressed rather than one who is liberated.

Lewis probably took himself and his comedy too seriously too soon – his straight performance in Martin Scorsese's *The King of Comedy* (1983) is, predictably, remarkable

and completely convincing – and his best films are not those directed by himself, but those directed by Frank Tashlin, like *The Disorderly Orderly*, and *It's Only Money* (1963). A former cartoonist, Tashlin calmly sidesteps the pretentious side of Lewis's persona and uses him as a brilliant creature to animate. In this, one is fleetingly reminded of another of the great movie comedy teams, Tom and Jerry, who in a series of scintillating Hanna Barbera car-

toons, took their feud not only to the point of high farce but even, in such gems as *The Cat Concerto* (1947) and *Johann Mouse* (1952), into the realms of high art.

'The high-tension comics like Jerry Lewis,' thought Mel Brooks, 'burn themselves out. It is the low-key laid-back comics like Jack Benny who are the ones that last.' Stan Laurel thought Benny 'a real craftsman who knows what consistent comedy characterization is.' Jack Benny's

BELOW: Jack Benny in *Charley's Aunt* (1941).

characterization was that of a mean, violin-playing narcissist who, as someone said, never *said* a bad word about anybody but did a lot of *thinking*. Like so many of the classic comedians, he mastered his craft in vaudeville and, although his film work does not always do him justice – perhaps his style was a little slow for the screwball era – we do have one classic screen performance from him, as the vain Shakespearean actor in war-torn Poland in Ernst Lubitsch's black comedy classic, *To Be or Not to Be* (1942). 'What you did to Hamlet,' he is told by a German Commandant

tress, and *International House* (1934), that Burns and Allen were seen to their best advantage. More recently, Burns made a remarkable comeback, after a 30-year absence from the screen, playing opposite Walter Matthau in *The Sunshine Boys* (1975) and winning himself an Oscar in the process for a performance that drew on a lifetime of comedy experience.

Clearly one can see that the legacy of all the great comedians celebrated in this book lives on. Mel Brooks pays homage to Chaplin and Jack Benny in his remake of the anti-Nazi satire, *To Be or Not to Be* (1982). Woody

LEFT: Not only following, but reveling, in the master's dance-steps: George Burns and Gracie Allen prove delightful dancing partners for Fred Astaire in *Damsel in Distress* (1937), directed by George Stevens.

bluntly, 'we are doing to Poland.'

From a somewhat similar background to Benny was George Burns, who starred in vaudeville, made his reputation in radio, and then made films with his wife Gracie Allen. He was the straight man to her scatterbrain. 'What date is it today?' she asks him at the beginning of *Damsel in Distress* (1937) and when he suggests that she look at the paper, she replies: 'That's no good, it's yesterday's paper.' It is in *Damsel in Dis-*

Allen apes the character of Bob Hope in his early career and then leans more to Chaplinesque pathos and artistic ambition later. The spirit of Harold Lloyd lives on in Jack Lemmon; of W C Fields in Walter Matthau; and Rod Steiger and Donald O'Connor have had a shot at playing Fields and Buster Keaton, respectively, in Hollywood biopics. At the time of writing, Sir Richard Attenborough is preparing his long-contemplated film about the life of Charlie

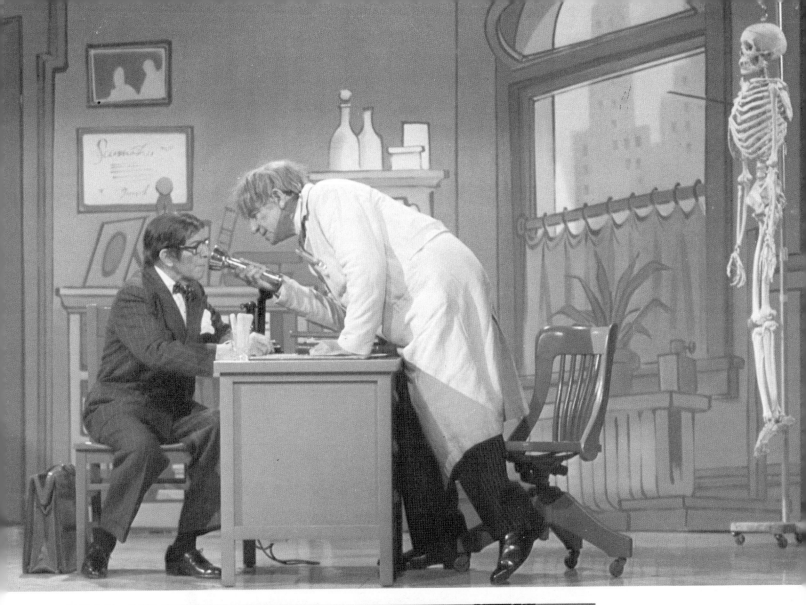

ABOVE: Feuding veterans: George Burns is threatened by his old vaudeville co-star Walter Matthau in the film of Neil Simon's *The Sunshine Boys*.

LEFT: A classic comedy team of the modern cinema: Jack Lemmon and Walter Matthau in *The Odd Couple* (1968).

RIGHT: Donald O'Connor as Buster Keaton in *The Buster Keaton Story* (1957), here seen in a recreation of a famous routine from *The Navigator*.

BELOW: Rod Steiger impersonates W C Fields in *W.C. Fields and Me* (1976).

Chaplin. Even here one can see that the survey is incomplete. A space should be made for a lady, Mae West, the Statue of Sexual Liberty who did for sex on screen what Cagney did for crime – that is, made it dangerously attractive – and therefore had to be toned down and censored before she had hit her stride. There is a separate volume still to be written about the movie comediennes, and indeed about feminist responses to the classic comedians.

'I hope this book is fun,' said Leonard Maltin about his valuable volume, *Movie Comedy Teams*, 'for after all, that's what comedy is all about.' Stan Laurel would have supported that and in many ways the comedies he made with Ollie Hardy represent the purest form of film fun: failure in all its forms, served with a complete lack of pretension. 'If laughter is what you're after,' said James Agee, 'then Harold Lloyd is your man, a country-hick extricating himself with delicious dexterity from ever-more absurd situations.' But comedy has claws too, and W C Fields and the Marx Brothers carry concealed stilettos to jab at the puffed-up pretensions of bourgeois life or officialdom, or anything that gave itself airs. With Buster Keaton, slapstick is given the grace of ballet, and with Chaplin

ABOVE: Chic Johnson (left) and Ole Olsen (right) in a moment from their classic of comedy lunacy, *Helzapoppin* (1941), a kind of forerunner of the Rowan and Martin *Laugh-In*.

LEFT: Bert Wheeler (left) and Robert Wolsey (center), one of the most successful of the vaudeville teams who were drawn to Hollywood by the talkies. Here seen in *The Nitwits* (1934), directed by George Stevens.

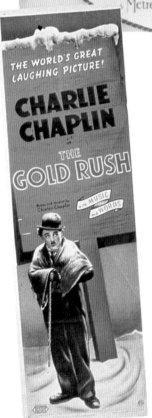

comedy acquires compassion and a conscience.

'What fools these mortals be!' says Puck in Shakespeare's *A Midsummer Night's Dream*. That is really what comedy is all about. We are all implicated in this judgment, which is the reason that comedy touches us all; and we are all fascinated by the different ways great comedians bring home this message to us. Fascinating to think how different comedians would have communicated Shakespeare's line: Chaplin with a resigned shrug perhaps, Groucho with a lascivious grin, Oliver Hardy with an air of misplaced pomp, W C Fields in a kind of muttered aside, Buster Keaton with a look. What is certain is that each, in his own way, would bring to it his own style and his own truth. In the end this is what makes their comedy 'classic': style and truth, unmistakable yet inimitable.

TOP, LEFT AND RIGHT: Three posters advertising three comedy classics: Laurel and Hardy's *Way Out West*, Chaplin's *The Gold Rush*, and The Marx Brothers' *A Day at the Races*.

INDEX

Page numbers *italics* refer to illustrations

ACKNOWLEDGMENTS

The author and publisher would like to thank the following people who helped in the preparation of this book: Alan Gooch, for his design and artwork; Nicki Giles for Production; Judith Millidge and Damian Knollys, the editors: and Ron Watson who compiled the index.

All pictures reproduced courtesy of **BPL**, except as follows: **The Bettmann Archive:** 1 (top left); 2 (top right); 7 (bottom); 20 (top); 24 (top); 27; 34; 36; 40; 41; 42; 45; 46; 48; 69 (top); 73; 77; 80; 82 (bottom); 83 (top); 84; 86; 87; 88 (top); 92; 103 (bottom); 123 (top); 124 (both); 125; 126 (both); 128; 129 (top); 131 (bottom); 132 (bottom); 133; 134 (both); 135 (both); 136 (top); 138; 139; 169 (bottom); 172 (both); 173 (bottom). **With co-Trustees of Harold Lloyd Trust A, 1985:** 1 (center left); 81 (top). **Library of Congress:** 14 (top).
Movie Star News/BPL: 167 (top).
Museum of Modern Art/Film Stills Archive, New York City: 3 (top left); 31; 56 (bottom); 57 (top); 63 (bottom); 64 (top); 170.
National Film Archive, London: 1 (top right); 2 (top left); 3 (top right); 9 (bottom); 11 (bottom left & right); 12 (both); 14 (bottom); 16 (bottom); 19; 20 (bottom); 22 (all); 25; 26; 29 (bottom); 32 (bottom); 44 (top); 47; 58 (bottom); 64 (bottom); 66; 74 (top); 76; 88 (bottom); 90; 97 (bottom); 103 (top); 143; 146 (top); 147; 148 (bottom); 150; 151 (bottom); 153; 154 (top); 155; 156 (top); 158 (bottom); 168; 174 (bottom left & right).
Jerry Ohlinger/Bison Archive: 167 (top).
Springer/Bettmann Film Archive: 18; 43; 53; 59 (top); 67; 69 (bottom); 82 (top); 91; 102; 120; 130; 131 (top); 136 (bottom).
Theater Collection, Museum of City of New York: 1 (center right).
Marc Wanamaker/BPL: 11 (top); 52; 68; 142.